PERFORMANCE IN A TIME OF TERROR

This volume is a collection of five Sinhala plays, translated into English, which were written and performed during the most violent phase of modern Sri Lankan history. Ranjini Obeyesekere's translation of these five well-known and celebrated plays by K.B. Herath, Prasannajith Abeysuriya, Dhananjaya Karunarathne, Prasanna Jayakody and Rajitha Dissanayake highlights and explores the dynamic period of Sri Lankan theater and performance arts in the 1980s and 1990s. The plays in this collection offered a political space for criticism, introspection, discussion and protest during a time of suppression of voices, political violence and terror. Audiences flocked to the theater to watch plays produced by talented dramatists and artists who were experimenting with forms and themes under extremely challenging circumstances, shoe-string budgets and strict censorship. Kanchuka Dharmasiri's introduction to the volume further details the history and socio-political contexts of the theater of this period, discussing themes such as dissent, identity and the brutal power of the state. She also looks at the unique formal elements employed in these plays as well as their influence and reach.

This volume is a significant addition to the growing corpus of Sinhala literature in translation. It will be an essential read for scholars and researchers of literature, performance studies, cultural studies, and the politics and history of Sri Lanka.

Ranjini Obeyesekere has a Ph.D. in English Literature from the University of Washington, Seattle. She has taught in the English Departments at the University of Peradeniya, Sri Lanka, and the University of California, San Diego. She also taught in the Department of Anthropology, Princeton University, for ten years before she retired. She has translated Sinhala prose and poetry for foreign and local journals, and anthologies. Her publications include *Sinhala Writing and the New Critics* (1974), *Jewels of the Doctrine: Translations from the Saddharmaratnāvaliya* (1991), *Sri Lankan Theater in a Time of Terror: Political Satire in a Permitted Space* (1999), *Portraits of Buddhist Women from the Sadharmaratnāvaliya* (2001), *Yasodhara: Wife of the Bodhisattva*

(2009) and *Sinhala Poetry in Translation* (2017). She is presently engaged in editing the third volume of the English translation of the fourteenth-century *Sinhala Jātaka Pot Vahansē*. Volumes 1 and 2 were published in 2012 and 2016 respectively.

Kanchuka Dharmasiri teaches in the Department of English at the University of Peradeniya, Sri Lanka, and her research interests include contemporary performance, translation and postcolonial studies. She has a Ph.D. in comparative literature from the University of Massachusetts, Amherst. Her articles and chapters have appeared in various journals and books such as *Translating Women: Different Voices and New Horizons* (2017), *Routledge Handbook of Asian Theatre* (2016), and *Mapping South Asia through Contemporary Theatre* (2014). She is the editor of *Streets Ahead with Haththotuwegama* (2013). Dharmasiri is also a theater director and translator. Her most recent production is *Nodutu Aes/Unseen Eyes* (2018/19), a devised multimedia play based on Bertolt Brecht and Kumari Kumaragamage's poetry.

PERFORMANCE IN A TIME OF TERROR

Five Sinhala Plays from Sri Lanka

Translated by Ranjini Obeyesekere

Edited by Kanchuka Dharmasiri

Routledge
Taylor & Francis Group
LONDON AND NEW YORK

First published 2021
by Routledge
2 Park Square, Milton Park, Abingdon, Oxon OX14 4RN

and by Routledge
52 Vanderbilt Avenue, New York, NY 10017

Routledge is an imprint of the Taylor & Francis Group, an informa business

British Library Cataloguing-in-Publication Data
A catalogue record for this book is available from the British Library

Library of Congress Cataloging-in-Publication Data
A catalog record has been requested for this book

ISBN: 978-0-367-54152-1 (hbk)
ISBN: 978-0-367-62515-3 (pbk)
ISBN: 978-1-003-10947-1 (ebk)

Typeset in Bembo

by SPi Global, India

CONTENTS

PHOTOGRAPHS

PREFACE

These five plays by Sri Lankan dramatists, some of them now recognized as major figures in the field, were translated by me around the time I was engaged in research in the late 1980s and 1990s and working on the book I later published as *Sri Lankan Theater in a Time of Terror: Political Satire in a Permitted Space: Sage 1999*. The plays were intended at the time to be a companion volume to that work.

After several years of research and a year and a half of total immersion in the theater world of Sri Lanka, awash at that time with plays by a host of creative, talented, young writers and directors, experimenting with different forms, styles, and themes and working on shoe string budgets, I was intrigued by the burgeoning theater audiences that crowded to these performances. They were not just audiences in Colombo but also in the provinces around the country. So much so that plays were actually making money and attracting more and more dramatists and actors into the performance world. Why this enormous interest in the theater and why now when censorship was so tight? Was it perhaps that people, strictly subjected to government controls and censorship, living in a world of anomie, political violence, abductions and terror, were grateful for the anonymity provided by a darkened auditorium to enjoy an evening's entertainment where the frustrations, pressures and political issues of the day could find expression in biting satire, creative comedy or sometimes in terrifying tragedies that were so close to experienced reality as to be perhaps cathartic in their impact? Or did the ephemeral nature inherent in a dramatic performance, the enormous flexibility in how an actor can shift, change or nuance a performance, provide the very immunity that the fixity of a book or painting or film could not have when faced with a censor board?

In exploring these issues and trying to understand why the theater could provide this political space especially during a period of heightened censorship, I began to look closely at a selection of plays and began to translate a few of them. However, on returning to teaching at the end of 1994, I barely had time to compete my book.

The translated plays, some of them only half done, got buried in my files and went into limbo. Now after over 20 years, talking to a young friend, a scholar and director of plays herself, and passionate about the world of performance and drama, I was urged to try to publish them with the promise that she would write an Introduction to place them in their context. So here they are for a younger generation of theater aficionados to enjoy as texts or revive and rework them in new and exciting forms.

Ranjini Obeyesekere
Kandy, August 2020

INTRODUCTION

Guns, coffins and existence: Five Sinhala plays from the 1980s and 1990s

The 1980s was one of the most violent periods in Sri Lanka's modern history, but, quite surprisingly, it was also a decade in which an unprecedented number of plays were produced in the island. A record number of 180 plays were produced in 1988 and 136 in 1989 as opposed to 40 plays in 1986 and 23 in 1987, for example.[1] Such a high number of theatrical productions in a single year was hitherto unheard-of. Ranjini Obeyesekere explores this phenomenon in *Sri Lankan Theater in a Time of Terror* (1999) and argues that even in the most dangerous and violent circumstances and challenging times in Sri Lanka, theater remained a vibrant and critical forum of expression and discussion. Theater continued to be a space that permitted a certain amount of protest and criticism. This does not imply that all plays were allowed to be performed or that there was no censorship. The large number of plays that seem to have escaped censorship or were being ignored by the censors remains a surprising factor.

During the same decade that Sri Lanka witnessed this dramatic upsurge in Sinhala theater, Tamil theater, especially after the 1983 anti-Tamil riots, became confined to the North and the East in stark contrast with previous years when Tamil theater was on par with Sinhala and English theater in the Colombo theater circles. Hence, if we are to trace the trajectories of the Sinhala, Tamil and English theater practices in Sri Lanka, they would take us in differential directions that intersect and diverge in certain points of time and space. This introduction will focus on Sinhala theater, because the five plays, which are translated into English, were written and performed in Sinhala.

Theater as a live performance art form holds a distinct place in many cultures, and, in the Sri Lankan context, theater has played a pivotal role in the formation of the postcolonial cultural fabric. One should likewise not forget that performances have been a significant part of the cultural makeup of the island since long before the advent of colonialism; many of these performances were connected to rituals and healing ceremonies. Hence, while colonialism and capitalism have affected the theatrical traditions in Sri Lanka—the introduction of the commercializing impulse to the arts, the adoption of European theatrical traditions, and the subsequent search for theatrical modes that address the new identity of the country—it did not indicate a definitive rupture from the older genres and traditions of ritual and other performances. Aparna Dharwadker's contention about Indian theater seems applicable to the Sri Lankan context too, in this instance. As she argues, "Indian theatrical modernity is at once inseparable from, and impossible to contain within, the parameters of Euro-modernity, because it represents the intersection of colonial and postcolonial processes with a much older, multilingual, multigeneric, indigenous, theater and performance culture."[2] It is true that Sri Lanka does not have the linguistic diversity that India possesses, but one does notice the ways in which postcolonial theater in Sri Lanka manifests "the intersection of colonial and postcolonial processes with a much older multilingual and multigeneric indigenous theatre and performance culture." In fact, Ediriweera Sarachchandra's creation of Maname, the play that marks a turning point in modern theater in Sri Lanka, entailed a process of experimentation that brought together European theatrics and indigenous performance genres. The desire to experiment and explore persist to this day and dramatists perform incredible feats of magic with minimal resources. In short, theater in Sri Lanka remains one of the most vibrant cultural activities in the country.

In the postcolonial context, an abundance of theater translations is taking place from a variety of languages into Sinhala and Tamil; yet, translational power dynamics are such that, while numerous plays from languages such as English, French or German are translated into Sinhala and Tamil, it is only rarely that a Sinhala or Tamil play gets translated into English or any other language. It is in such a context that these translations by Ranjini Obeyesekere open up a space for the English language reader to engage in and converse with five Sinhala plays written and performed in the 1980s and the 1990s. Hence, this collection offers an invaluable addition to the corpus of translated Sinhala literature and a significant source for those who search for theater scripts that one cannot read in the original languages. In fact, this is the first time that a collection of five Sinhala plays translated into English is brought together in a single volume. These plays capture and question dominant social, economic and political narratives of the times and explore the place of the human being in a society ravaged by the violence of commercialism, the brutality of the state and centralized power politics.

To understand the contextual specificities of these plays, it would be useful to pay attention to the pivotal transformations that took place in Sri Lanka from the late 1970s to the 1990s. One decisive systemic change that affected society and life in Sri Lanka is the liberalization of the economy in 1977. With the new economic system where the state focused on securing the market and private investment thereby curtailing the benefits of social welfare in the process, together with the creation of private enterprises in urban spaces, the country saw a rapid migration of youth from villages to the city, in the hope of procuring employment and achieving glittery middle-class dreams. Yet, most of them lived in squalid conditions, surviving on a bare minimum. The suppression of the general strike in 1981, the anti-Tamil violence in 1983, the onset of the war that would last for almost 30 years, and the second JVP[3] led youth insurrection from 1987 to 1989 marked the 1980s. The centralization of power with the executive presidency, established in 1978 during the rule of the United National Party lead by J.R. Jayawardena, also affected society in insidious ways. Likewise, censorship of the arts, the curtailment of free speech and the practice of arresting citizens as "terrorists" became prevalent in these times. The Emergency State became the norm rather than an exception. Enforced disappearances of youth and journalists increased. The last few years of the decade witnessed the brutal killing of thousands of young men and women in the state's attempt to repress the second youth insurrection led by the JVP.[4] The brutality of the state and counter-state violence took a public face as burning bodies of young men and women were displayed in public spaces. The display of dead and tortured bodies turned into a day-to-day event as people grew increasingly apprehensive of speaking openly about the situation. At the same time, in 1987, the Indo-Lanka Accord was signed and the Indian Peace Keeping Forces arrived in the North and East of the country.

Compared to the seventies and eighties, the post-1994 period brought about a time of relative calm in the South. President Chandrika Kumarathunga came to power with the promise of peace and prosperity, ending an era of state and non-state violence and quelling the fear psychosis that prevailed after the armed suppression of the JVP. Discussions for a peaceful political solution to the national question commenced between the government of Sri Lanka and Liberation Tigers of Tamil Elam (LTTE); however, the peace negotiation between the two parties lasted only a year, and another round of war began in 1995. The violence affected the lives of millions of people. In the political economic sphere, for the first time in its history the Sri Lanka Freedom Party officially acknowledged the viability of free market economic reforms—with slogans such as "a market with a human face"—where the United National Party had so far been identified as the pioneering force.

This is merely a cursory glance at some of the pivotal social events that mark the decades extending from the 1970s to the 1990s. The five plays in this collection are written during this period: K.B. Herath's *Māyā Dēvi/ Goddess of Illusion* in 1984, Prasannajith Abeysuriya's *Dukgannārāla/ Bearer of Woes* in 1989, Dhananjaya Karunarathne's *Jūriya/ The Jury* and Prasanna Jayakody's *Sevanäli saha Minissu/ Shadows and Men* in 1993 and Rajitha Dissanayake's *Mata Veditiyannädda? / Aren't You Going to Shoot Me?* in 1999. These plays observe, comment on, and critique the happenings of these three decades in a variety of ways. By bringing out the voices of characters from different class backgrounds and gendered positions, the plays interrogate dominant social, economic and political narratives.

Māyā Dēvi/The Goddess of Illusion by K.B. Herath (1984)

K.B. Herath, a veteran theater director and playwright began his theatrical career in the late 1960s. His plays, which often combine traditional performance methods with more realistic theatrical techniques, bring onto stage retellings of historical narratives and portrayals of contemporary life. Framed by a group of goddesses, gods and demons, Herath's play *Goddess of Illusion*, at one level, is about a family that owns a funeral parlor and the parents, Mudalāli,[5] the profit-driven businessman, and his wife who are desperate to marry off their psychologically and physically disabled daughter, Lakshmi. Singularly motivated by a desire to procure a husband for their daughter who no longer can navigate the world in a socially accepted way, they fail to recognize the human factor in those whom they manipulate in order to secure their goal. Hence, Sugath, Mudalāli's nephew, a former Buddhist monk who is forced to disrobe and abandon his religious order to manage the funeral parlor, and Mudalāli's sister, Denagama Hāminē, become mere pawns in the wealthy family's preplanned game. One should also note that the prevailing feudal order and hierarchical relationships intersect with the capitalist system thus doubly binding those who are economically dependent on wealthy landowners and/or businessmen. The wife, perhaps the only one-dimensional character in a play that otherwise presents an array of complex characters, speaks about Sugath as if he is an inanimate object, something trivial and expendable. In fact, when they realize that Lakshmi's physical and psychological well-being has improved as a result of her association with Sugath, they immediately plan her marriage to a lawyer, a connection that would enable them to ascend the social ladder. Here, Lakshmi, too, becomes a mere pawn in their game. By deceiving Sugath, the parents are deceiving their own daughter, and she succumbs to her insanity again.

Goddess of Illusion was written in 1984, seven years after the liberalization of the economy, and the play explores the intersection of neocolonial, capitalist and feudal politics that affect the lives of two generations of characters. The continuation of the colonial capitalist set-up in the postcolonial context is made clear when Mudalāli reminiscences about the way in which he inherited the coffin business from Jonklass, a Britisher. Under the sign "Jonklass Undertakers" where coffins are stacked one upon the other, Mudalāli and his employees, Newton and Simon, wait for news of death, the only news that is able to energize and enliven these men. By asserting, "You can't wait around trying to figure out when you are going to die. If you want to survive in these times you must find out when others are going to die," Mudalāli disclaims any space for introspection. It is with pride that he recalls the days when he had the most sales: "During the malaria epidemic there were days when I sold over a hundred coffins. Ah! When will a time like that ever come again!" According to Mudalāli, the coffins have become a part of himself; he embodies their essence and is unable to perceive a reality that exists outside of the coffins and the profit associated with them. He, as the owner of the coffin business, is in the higher stratum in the system while characters such as Simon, who is disfigured physically as a result of electrocution, serves as a constant reminder of those who are victimized by this exploitative system. Speaking about the play, K.B. Herath states the following: "no one would say that the prosperity that is needed for a human being's existence is unnecessary. Yet, isn't mere prosperity which lacks intelligence and ethics an insanity?"[6] The dramatic shift in the way people relate to each other in the new context and its consequent perversions are thrown into poignant relief in the play.

Amidst these characters, one finds the estranged and alienated Lakshmi. Through Lakshmi's character—a woman on the fringe of society and sanity—the play offers another potent critique of the repercussions that the capitalist system has on human beings. Lakshmi constantly speaks of her childhood among the coffins and sings the lines "Here a coffin, there a coffin,/Everywhere a coffin, coffin." She sees through the artificial workings of the system and perceives the horror in its raw form. She opens up to Sugath when she states,

> Ever since I was a child everyone has appeared to me as a demon. All around me were coffins. Amidst those coffins the only person who seemed human was your mother. […] I don't remember what happened to me in the recent past. But now I know that I'm once again, just a lonely cripple, lost among these coffins and corpses.

Lakshmi has grown up among the coffins, among those who eagerly wait for news of death; she cannot remain sane in a setting where emotions and feelings are deemed redundant while profit and gain are considered to be the only desirable traits. As a sensitive young woman, she opts to escape the system by creating her own imaginary fantasy world, which is temporarily interrupted by Sugath's love and compassion. Nevertheless, quite ironically, Lakshmi's fantastical musings are also couched in neoliberal parlance; hence, it is to Singapore and Japan that she travels with her little furry animal Arya.

According to Gamini Haththotuwegama, a playwright and critic, "K.B. Herath is a dramatist who is a grim, macabre, sardonic excavator of unpleasant and submerged 'truths' about family, marriage, women, and religion. He is a good debunker, unafraid to prise open the hypocrisy, greed and ambition of the local priesthood."[7] In fact, while providing a scathing critique of the workings of the family by examining the exploitative and manipulative relationship between parents, children and relatives, *Goddess of Illusion* also scrutinizes the role of religion in the new political economic order. The reference to the disrobed young monk who migrated and became a plumber is an indication of the ways in which people tried to negotiate the new socio-economic order; it also implies that plumbing might be a more lucrative business than religion. One is given the sense that Sugath, too, had entered the Buddhist order for pragmatic reasons, partly because of his economic difficulties. Yet even Sugath, who is ambivalent about taking over the management of the funeral home, ultimately falls prey to the system.

At the same time, the migration of the ex-monk to take up employment as a plumber refers to the mass labor migrations—especially as domestic workers and laborers to the Middle East to work in often unwholesome conditions—that took place in the 1980s. Such migration is also part of Sarasvathi's family. She speaks of her brother, an actor, who had to migrate for employment because he was unable to make a living in Sri Lanka as an artist. In what ends up as a tragedy, her brother dies abroad, and his body is sent home. Saraswathi laments, "He came in a box, wrapped in foil, on a bed of ice and sawdust … Since that day coffins disgust me, so does money!" Saraswathi wants to be a musician and is not interested in the monetary dreams that many others are invested in. The difficulty of doing art in the new economic context is referred to in a few other instances in the play as well. Speaking of a fresh corpse that is brought to the funeral home, Newton asserts, "He's a famous artist. There's nothing left of him to embalm, however. Hardly an ounce of flesh on the poor guy!" The humor in the statement makes us laugh and the play is replete with such darkly humorous moments; yet, at times such instances are unsettling. Writing about the play, Ediriweera Sarachchandra states that "the audience laughs, but at the bottom of their hearts they know they shouldn't laugh and cannot laugh."[8]

Goddess of Illusion illustrates the double bind of exploitation where the new capitalist order overlaps with an older hierarchical feudal order and enables Mudalāli and the like to exert enormous power over people such as Denagama Hāminē and Sugath. Their lives do not matter; they are poor. I am reminded of a Bertolt Brecht poem, "Song of Commodity"[9]:

> Do I know what Man is?
> How should I know who should know?
> I don't know what Man is.
> All I know is his price.

In *Goddess of Illusion*, the man that Mudalāli knows is the dead man. He knows the price of the dead man only too well, but in the process of becoming a very part of the coffins that he sells and therefore implicitly a part of the world of the dead, he loses awareness of the living and breathing human beings around him, and along with it a sense of his own humanity.

Dukgannārāla/The Bearer of Woes (1989) by Prasannajith Abeysuriya

The ways in which people of the lower strata in the working class deal with the consequences of the Capitalist system is an issue that Parasannajith Abeysuriya addresses in *The Bearer of Woes*. The young woman in the play has resorted to prostitution as a final bid for survival while the unemployed man lives with a continuously deferred dream of a transformed society. The play captures their struggles and illustrates how the woman's situation is worse than the man's when the factor of gender is added to the equation. Her burden only gets exacerbated by the man's arrival and the main conflict between the two characters lies in the fact that the man, who dreams of changing the future, remains oblivious of the woman's plight and is not cognizant of the fact that he, too, contributes to further it.

The play was staged in a time when state terror was at its height and one can see how the play questions some of the ideas embraced by the young rebels. Though the man in the play has lofty dreams of transforming society, he is not exactly aware of the practicalities of everyday existence. Hence, he tells the woman that she needs to be patient till he finishes his book without considering the fact that she is desperate to feed two children. Hence, though the man perceives himself as the bearer of woes, the bearer of the society's woes, it is the woman who becomes the bearer of woes at a pragmatic level. The translation of this play was originally published in Ranjini Obeyesekere's *Sri Lankan Theater in a Time of Terror*, and the following section is taken from the translator's note. It provides a clear idea of the title and the concept of the play:

> In the courts of the kings of Sri Lanka there was an official known as Dukgannārāla. The word literally meant "the gentleman who takes on burdens or woes." He was a kind of ombudsman who heard the people's complaints and brought them to the king's notice. He was also a kind of scapegoat. In this play, the "Man" takes on the burdens of the downtrodden and so is a self-appointed Dukgannārāla; but the woman ironically becomes the real "bearer of woes." The dramatist clearly plays with both ideas.[10]

The man's conception of the world—where he has the freedom and space to self-define himself as a bearer of woes—and the inevitable role that the woman has to play as the bearer of woes in day to day life, is brought into contrast in the play.

The Bearer of Woes begins with a group of singers and dancers on stage. A few minutes after their performance commences, one hears a commotion at the side entrance and a woman enters carrying a child. She is running away from a man who has physically abused her and is seeking refuge in the theater. Subsequently, the man enters the scene and immediately takes over the narrative, purporting to tell "our story." With a tinge of righteousness, he recounts that he "saved" the woman from her previous life as a sex worker. What he omits in his narrative is the way in which the woman became more disempowered as a result and was left with more mouths to feed. He claims, "Until my book is completed we will all have to suffer for just a while longer. You should put up with this and be a little patient." This statement made at the end of the play illustrates that his convictions remain unchanged.

What we hear in the play is fundamentally the man's story. We hear the woman's story through the man's perspective. Since the couple cannot reach a consensus, the performers enact "Vessanthara Jātakaya," where the Bodhisattva gives away his wife and children in his journey to attain enlightenment.[11] Vessanthara Jātakaya has often been used as an example to illustrate the ideal wife/woman who would support the husband in any circumstance. After the enactment of the play, the woman gets bombarded with moralizing advice. Having had an excess of it, she questions:

> Why does everyone blame me? Didn't I suffer in silence all these months? One fellow left me pregnant, abandoned me and ran away. Another promised me kingly comforts but what did I get? Nothing! If we ate one meal, we starved all next day. No money for an illness, for essential medicines. The child's schooling

> had to stop. To add to everything, I now have to cope with his temper and fear for my life. I'm worse off than I was. That's the only difference.

The woman breaks the silence as she questions the moral of the religious story as well as the blame directed at her, thereby critiquing the dominant patriarchal worldview.

In the final part of the play, the performers and the director, who by this time are weary of the man's ideas about social equality and transformation, conclude that he is not "normal," and the troupe performs an exorcism ceremony to eliminate some presumed demon of social equality that has possessed the man. The ceremony is replete with images of violence and social and economic disparity. Images such as "Mounds of skeletons appear/Graves sprout along the roads," and "The fires of hunger burn fierce and bright/Wives are sent to far off lands as sacrifice," respectively refer to the terror of the late eighties and then the migration of women as housemaids to bring in foreign remittances to the island. We already came across references to the labor migrations and will encounter images of skeletons and grave yards in other plays included in this volume. The man, after the exorcising ceremony, refuses to be defeated and asks the woman to come back with him. He does not seem to have undergone any change in his views. The woman does not respond to his request for her to return. Her silence leaves the ending of the play ambiguous and open.

Jūriya/The Jury by Dhananjaya Karunarathne

The events in *The Jury* unravel through the actions of Manuvansa, who, having been brought up in an isolated children's home, is clueless about the workings of the socio-economic system. His positionality enables him to see and experience systemic injustice at a rather visceral level. *The Jury* was staged in 1993 when a certain space was opened up for public discussion, though the violence in the late 1980s had not yet completely subsided. The play, using elements of the absurdist genre as well as Bertolt Brecht's theatrics, responds to the events that occurred in the preceding years, while probing audiences to engage with questions related to silence and complicity.

In a Kafkaesque moment, Manuvansa[12] discovers an amputated leg in a garbage heap and is aghast while everyone around him treats the incident as an ordinary occurrence. It is Manuvansa's first day at work as a municipal worker and the opening conversation between him and his co-workers foreshadows one of the main thematic concerns of *The Jury*. When asked for his opinion about the new job, Manuvansa claims that it is good "but a little smelly." In response, his co-worker, Bahitē states that "At first, we also felt that way. After a while all smells and scents disappear." This statement has larger significations when analyzed in relation to the particular socio-political context in which the play was performed. Recall that the latter part of the eighties made a spectacle of violence as dead and tortured bodies were displayed in public spaces. The State of Emergency created a tense atmosphere in which anyone could get arrested without a warrant and could be detained for weeks. There were instances of journalists and writers who likewise "disappeared"; freedom of speech was curtailed. In this context, violence was normalized and made a part of everyday existence; citizens were desensitized to the smell of blood and the sight of dead bodies and body parts.

Therefore, for the characters in *The Jury*, the appearance of a human limb is "normal," and they have ceased to question it, or rather the system has trained them to assume an attitude of indifference because questioning all but criminalizes the inquirer or in fact ensures that she or he is silenced permanently. Manuvansa's dilemma is twofold: for one, he is unable to gauge the general fear in the atmosphere that compels certain characters such as his co-workers to remain silent in the face of what he discovers, and, on the other hand, he does not comprehend the ways in which the authority figures intentionally work to ensure that the truth remain unexposed. Insidious politics and ideology are at play here. Again, Brecht:

> For to say that something is natural
> In [...] times of bloody confusion
> Of ordained disorder, of systematic arbitrariness
> Of inhuman humanity is to
> Regard it as unchangeable.[13]

The defeatist notion of the unchangeability of social and political circumstances was apparent in the normalization of state violence. Since it was customary to see dead and burning bodies in the streets and people were apprehensive of asking questions, Manuvansa's quest for the truth is seen as an anomaly. The title of the play itself is an ironic manifestation of the socio-political situation in the late-1980s, which was marked by the absence of "a jury" or anyone to bear witness to the delivering of justice.

Manuvansa is shocked by the discovery of the leg and equally shocked by the absolute indifference of the police officers when he arrives at the police station to report it. Upon realizing that there is no personal gain for Manuvansa in his pursuit of justice, Hencharāla, states, "Man, if there is nothing you want personally and this is not your problem, take that stinking shovel and get out of here." Hencharāla's perspective holds sway among a majority of characters. Manuvansa's co-workers realize his honest intentions, but knowing the system, try to dissuade him from further inquiry. In an attempt to distract Manuvansa, the police officer offers outlandish explanations of the situation:

> You are a madman. I have never in my whole life met such a pest as you. Why you son of a bitch, you spend all this money, pursuing a matter that is no concern of yours. Didn't you know we even put an "ad" in the papers saying, "Found a leg. Let the owner please report to the security division."

Though reminiscent of Nikolai Gogol's "Nose," where Kovalyov places an ad in a newspaper in a desperate attempt to find his vagrant nose, unlike the satire in Gogol's short story, the implications in *The Jury* are more macabre. The policeman's refusal to give serious consideration to Manuvansa's complaint, signify a certain amount of complicity of the state institutions in the violent happenings in the country. The treatment meted out to Manuvansa is also a commentary on class politics, which is particularly apparent when contrasted with the way in which Englesina, the high-class woman from Colombo, and her dog are treated.

The Jury offers a scathing critique of the public institutions in the country: police, law, and religion. Vahansē, the religious figure, manipulates Manuvansa's goodwill and honesty in order to extract money from him by performing various rituals on behalf of the man who lost his leg. This religious man, who in the beginning exchanges his older pistol for a new one, capitalizes on Manuvansa's conscience. The lawyer, too, contrives to rob Manuvansa of his minimal possessions and has no qualms in allowing Manuvansa to mortgage his house to procure the lawyer's fee. He "shouts for joy" as he tells his wife, "Our life is going to change now. I promise you from now on we will not have to suffer living in rented houses. We can have a child."

Such absurdist moments are juxtaposed with the brutal violence that was ravaging the country. The graphic image of the leg, tortured and violated, remains a concrete presence:

> This leg is a man's leg. It has been separated from the man's body at the knee. At the place where it was severed there are burn marks, bruise marks, marks of an explosive, scratch marks, marks of having been smashed by the tires of a vehicle, ant bite marks, dog bite marks, marks of a dog having pissed on it and several other marks that cannot be identified.

This gruesome description alludes to the many layers of cruelty and violence inflicted on the human body. Not only has the young man between 25 and 30 been tortured in a variety of brutal methods, but after the torture and potential murder, he has also been left to the mercy of dogs and ants. Throughout the play, the characters are discouraged from paying close attention to the factual details of the actual crime. What happens, rather, is a systematic erasure of the crime, done in a very deliberate manner with the involvement of many players in the state, security and judicial system. The leg is a kind of synecdoche not only for the tortured man, but for a nation of people suffering violence.

The Jury has two possible endings.[14] When Manuvansa realizes that he will gain no backing for his cause from the characters in the play, he pleads for the support of the audience members. Participatory theater was not a commonly practiced genre in Sri Lanka in the early 1990s and hence the director was surprised when an audience member walked on to the stage in support of Manuvansa in one of the early performances. Ranjini Obeyesekre claims, "Both the director and the actors were momentarily stunned and did not know how to proceed. It was at this point that the director brought the play to a brilliant close with the gunshot and a quick curtain."[15] This incident speaks of the challenges and the sheer imagination that is required during a live performance event. In the earlier version, Manuvansa returns from prison and is a transformed man. He is abusive and violent towards his wife, Sunvunā, perhaps the least developed character in the play and who seems to be present only to be exploited and abused. Most of all, he has learned to comply with the system. If Eugène Ionesco's *Rhinoceros* shows the way in which individual characters, one by one, transform into rhinoceroses and how an entire population ends up becoming thick-skinned beasts, Manuvansa in *The Jury* learns to ignore the violence and injustice directed at ordinary men and women. *Rhinoceros* was written in the context of growing popular support for fascism in Europe—Ionesco was particularly appalled by the rise of the Iron Guard in Rumania—while *The Jury* was performed in the context of the normalization of state violence in its various manifestations. The portrayal of the ease with which violence could be disregarded, and the way in which people become inured to such heinous acts through systemic mechanisms, is what makes this play a powerful commentary on the time of fear and terror in the 1980s.

Sevanäli saha Minissu/Shadows and Men by Prasanna Jayakody

Prasanna Jayakody's *Shadows and Men* was staged in the same year as *The Jury* and though seemingly different from the other plays presented in this volume, it has overlapping themes and concerns. *Shadows and Men* is more of a meditation on life, an exploration of the internal workings of the human psyche juxtaposed with the external circumstances that affect existence. The beginning of the play resembles a painting that gradually transforms into a moving picture. Through the shadowy yellowish lights, we see Dungura (Everyman) slowly rise to his feet and search for Dungu, his mind, who, after some time, appears from the rear of the theater, with a rope tied around his waist. He is pulled along the center aisle of the auditorium by Dungu who holds the other end of the rope. The two are tied to each other by the rope. This appears to be Dungura's first experience of the disconnect between mind and body as he tells Dungu: "I have looked for you throughout my entire body but you are not there. Ever since you were a little child you never left my sight." Yet, Dungura is now a young man and Dungu, unknown to Dungura, has journeyed distances that Dungura is unable to travel physically. The surreal and the real intersect; "this work experimentalizes many things," comments Gamini Haththotuwegama, paying special attention to the first scene. He further asserts, "Its use of a grotesque stage setup, a rope hanging in the centre of the auditorium on which emerges the protagonist, struggling, sensationalizes the action."[16] Dungura, then, puts on a tie—he is now a part of the work force— and gets on the train with Dungu; they scrutinize the thoughts and movements of the other passengers as the play seeks answers to fundamental questions about existence.

In the ensuing scene Dungura/Dungu meets Chukkina/Chukki (Everywoman) at a crucial juncture in her life, a moment after her attempted suicide. What has driven Chukkina/Chukki to attempt to take her own life is a desperate feeling of loneliness and hopelessness. The first conversation Chukkina and Dungura have is about god. It is unclear what draws them together; perhaps it is their profound loneliness or a more instinctual sexual desire. After their sexual encounter, Dungu and Chukki theorize about passion, its satiation and childbirth while their union brings forth multiple children who are sent out to the world—"an endless desert out there with no road"—to become good citizens.

As the two grow old and physically weak, "[swinging] back and forth between boredom and pain" like "the ticking of the clock," they wait for their grown-up children to visit them, an expectation that only ends up in disappointment. Though the children do not return, Dungu and Chukki refuse to let go of their hope. They are burdened by thoughts of loneliness and isolation as they hope against hope. The bodies are old now; the minds make requests with which the bodies can no longer comply. "I am lonely, I am lonely, I am lonely" cries Chukkina, unable to bear the burden of loneliness. Chukki strangles her. The children return to their mother's funeral, but depart when they are informed that their mother did not leave them any material possessions. Chukki hovers around after Chukkina's demise and later on disappears into the sack. Dungu's utterance that "A clock ticks for no particular purpose. It keeps going for as long as it is wound," is the first indication that human life might be as directionless and mechanical as the movements of a clock. Towards the end of the play, unable to figure out whether the time is six in the morning or the evening, Dungu claims, "The clock is right. There is nothing now left to add to our lives. Today there is no difference between us and the clock." For Dungu, they have arrived at the end of their life cycle and hence must supersede the concept of time. Reminiscent of the opening scene, Dungu is no longer in sight when Dungura meets his end.

What is the purpose of life? The Sisyphean task of pushing the boulder up the hill and then rolling it back up again and again resonates with the image of people going to work before sunrise and returning after the sun has set: "People are running back. Their faces are despairing. There's not a smile on anyone's face" observes Dungu. Dungura and Chukkuni seem happy as they go through the motions of accepted social life: marriage, procreation and the raising of children to become good citizens of the land. But what happens after? What is the purpose of it all? What is the meaning of life? In *The Myth of Sisyphus* Albert Camus tells us that we should imagine Sisyphus happy as he takes the boulder up the hill. Jayakody, the playwright asserts, "Life is built on expectations. We make a bundle of our dearest hopes and spend our whole life trying to realize them. In that search we engage in numerous absurd, meaningless acts. When those expectations are unrealizable men try to build their lives yet again on various other expectations." The process is never-ending. The play captures the samsaric cycle of existence.

Shadows and Men is abstract, but also absurd at some levels, especially in relation to the dialogues that take place between Dungura, Chukkini and their minds. For example, the following conversation is akin to something that one would find in Beckett's *Waiting for Godot* or Eugène Ionesco's *The Bald Soprano*:

DUNGURA: People in the insane asylum have put up a board saying that everyone outside is mad.

DUNGU: Mosquitoes that sing a song in your ear and then suck your blood are everywhere.
DUNGURA: They have put up a sign on the main public road saying it is a private family burial ground.
DUNGU: Look! Look! Nero has come here too to play his fiddle.

These lines at first glance may appear to make little sense, but upon careful scrutiny one can see how each line relates or comments on a significant socio-cultural or political event or sentiment of the times or how they become part of a larger philosophical inquiry. What is madness? If "People in the insane asylum have put up a board saying that everyone outside is mad," what, in fact, are those who are outside engaged in? While in the train, Dungura asks Dungu, "Even before the sun can kiss the earth people are awake. Where are they running in this dark?" Dungu responds as follows: "They have got up early to start their struggle with life. They have no time to sit around and think, to be happy, to make love. Look at them. They don't have even a shadow of a thought." Dungura here notices people who run incessantly, without thinking, in a rat-race that has transformed them into machines. If each man in T.S. Eliot's "The Waste Land" set in the 1920s industrial England "fixed his eyes before his feet"— "I had not thought death had undone so many" contemplates one speaker in the poem—the people in Jayakody's *Shadows and Men* have "no smiles on their faces" and "don't have even a shadow of a thought." Alienated labor and constant work have estranged human beings from their own selves.

Going back to the four lines that I quoted in the beginning of the previous paragraph, the second instance where there is mention of a sign, this one put up in "the public road saying it is a private family burial ground," makes sinister references to the violence of the latter part of the 1980s. In fact, one of the dominant traits of the state violence of the period between 1987 and 1989 was the public display of tortured and dead bodies. The state thus performed its power making it clear to the public as to what would ensue if one refused to comply with authority. Hence, public land was a mass burial ground that the politicians used as their own private property.

What is remarkable about Jayakody's play is the way in which the social and political inquiry intersects with the more metaphysical questions about life, death, god, expectations and existence. Hence, at one level, we see Dungura and Chukkuni meeting, getting married and having many children who all leave the parents only to return to Chukkuni's funeral. We also witness their pain and longing as they wait for their children to return. I agree with Haththotuwegama when he asserts that "There are many shades of Becket (*Endgame*, arguably)," in Jayakody's play, and see how it resonates with another Beckett play, *Waiting for Godot* as well as Eugène Ionesco's *Chairs*, where the process of waiting becomes a central trope. Waiting is connected with expectations and hope. Initially, the parents hope that the children will eventually take care of them and then go through a process of incessant waiting, till their bodies ache. There is a sense of waiting that permeates the play, waiting for the mind to connect with the body, waiting for the children to come back, and then finally waiting for the end of life.

Mata Veḍitiyannädda?/Aren't You Going to Shoot Me?

Rajitha Dissanayake's *Aren't You Going to Shoot Me?* takes us into Upul and Ravi's small room with a window. Similar to *Shadows and Men*, the setting is urban and the two characters are almost room-bound as a result of the political situation in the country. Upul is an unemployed young man trying to make ends meet with odd jobs such as selling cellular phones; Ravi is a university student who gets a certain amount of support from his parents. They have been constantly shifting rooms to evade discontented landlords. The two manage with a bare minimum, but Upul's family is under the impression that he leads a comfortable life in the city; he is one among many young men and women who migrated to the city with hopes for employment and a better future. In the bleak situation where the two young men do not even know where to find money to pay rent, they take refuge in ogling the legs of a woman in an adjoining building. The play captures a certain sense of hopelessness and apathy brought about by the aftermath of the time of terror and the uncertainty created by the war between the Sri Lankan state and the LTTE that escalated in the latter part of the 1990s. The feeling of hopelessness connects to politics at a global level as well, especially with the shock and uncertainty created by the dissolution of the Soviet Union in 1991, which had serious repercussions on the leftist movements all around the world. Many young people were affected by the disillusionment caused by this event, which put dreams of a socialist future on hold. Hence, the claustrophobic atmosphere in the play, where Upul and Ravi are literally trapped in a room, also connects to a larger sense of an impasse. Where do they go from here?

At the same time, the Prevention of Terrorism Act, which was introduced in the late 1980s in order to suppress the JVP insurrection, was implemented again in the late 1990s and an emergency state was announced, thus enabling the police and the military to arrest and question any person without prior notice. Though the situation was calm in the first few years of Chandrika Bandaranayaka's presidency, violence again became a pervasive factor in the latter part of the decade. It is because of such tight surveillance and security that Upul is unable to return the day's earnings to his manager, which makes him lose his temporary job. Hence, not only is Upul economically desperate, but his situation is exacerbated by the fact that he is unable to navigate public spaces with a sense of safety for his eclectic business enterprises. His class status as an unemployed man contributes to the way in which he is perceived by others.

Part of the anxiety that Upul and Ravi feel can be attributed to this general mood in the country. The chaos of their lives and the reality around them is captured when Upul asserts, "Did you know that a bomb went off near the clock tower today? Many died they say. In the middle of all that our guys have lost the game. There is a rumor that tomorrow the buses are going on strike." On the one hand, people in the South were becoming cognizant of the war as bombs started exploding in public spaces and transport systems in the South. With that awareness, the imminence of death and the transience of life was made all the more clear. At the same time, acts such the Prevention of Terrorism Act allowed the police and the military to arrest anyone without a warrant, and hence the anxiety of young men like Upal around venturing out into public spaces. In Upul's statement, the exploding bombs and the human causalities are juxtaposed with the cricket match, which seemed to lull citizens into momentarily forgetfulness of the violent realities around them or issues such as unemployment or the struggles for higher wages.

If the current socio-political context does not provide the young men any prospect of a viable future, what options do they have? Lost in a world where they have no control over their external circumstances, or as a matter of fact their own lives, Upul writes love letters and gives the same letter to different women while Ravi ogles the legs of a wealthy young woman in an adjoining building. Soon, Upul, too, joins Ravi in observing the woman's legs; they obsess over her; she seems to stand for something that they long for. Critic and writer, Liyanage Amarakeerthi claims,

> Those legs are a kind of window to a world of happiness that they otherwise cannot afford. For one of the men, the legs are the point of departure for his imaginary world of pleasure and a beautiful distraction from frustrating realities of life. He keeps watching them from a distance.[17]

Their voyeuristic pastime illustrates their sexual desires and frustrations while it is also intricately connected to their aspirations of class mobility. Their desire is not for just any woman but for an upper-class woman with beautiful white legs, who dances, and who even has a private driver to take her shopping in Bambalapitiya and Kollupitiya, some of the expensive shopping areas.

The disillusionment of life that becomes manifest in the dealings in the public space is also reflected in personal relationships. One almost feels that Upul has lost his ability to connect with people deeply when he speaks of the act of giving the same love letter to multiple girlfriends. Though meant as a playful gesture and an attempt to demonstrate his masculine prowess, this statement is also a commentary on the breakdown of relationships and human connections. Interestingly though, the relationships that take place in their fantasy world are also riddled with ambiguity and disconnectedness. They manifest the young men's desire for upward social mobility, but within that mobility, they form no deep bond; in fact, the fantasies are rampant with stereotypes such as the one of the nagging wife who constantly complains about financial issues. In the fantasy, too, Upul manages to sustain multiple relationships and justifies his conduct by telling Dhammi, Ravi's wife with whom he seems to be having an affair, that "Men are like that." Mired in bills, dissatisfaction, and deception, the fantasy unfortunately does not offer much that is different from their present state of existence.

If *Shadows and Men* embodies a certain sense of waiting, both literal and metaphysical, *Aren't You Going to Shoot Me?* depicts a very concrete process of waiting where the two men seem to be trapped in a room with almost no access to the outside world. It is not that they are not allowed to navigate public spaces, but what is telling is the fact that they feel anxious to venture out as a result of the prevailing socio-political situation. Unemployed and financially unstable, they are almost forced into a life of stasis. We hardly hear of Ravi leaving the room—university students were particularly targeted during the 1987–1989 period—but often witness him on his bed, staring out a window that serves as the only outlet for his dreams. Unlike the brooding Ravi, Upul is more of a doer and in a competitive vein tries to approach the woman through her driver, which proves to be a misguided effort on his part. The two seem to be engaged in a certain amount of imagination and play as they try to pass the days, pass time. In Beckett's *Waiting for Godot*, after Lucky and Pozzo leave the scene, Vladimir claims, "That passed the time," to which Estragon responds, "It would have passed in any case." Upul and Ravi are not exactly Vladimir and Estragon, but they are waiting, waiting for some sort of salvation or hope. Yet, the circumstances that they have to face are challenging because, as Upul claims, "Whatever one tries to do one always ends up getting beaten. That's all that happens." The sheer uncertainty and the terror that prevailed among a certain group of youth, the indecision and ambiguity about life, is captured in *Aren't You Going to Shoot Me?*

A note on gender

There were almost 500 plays produced in the 1980s and 1990s. In total, 499 of the plays were written and directed by men. There was a single female playwright and director in their midst, Somalatha Subasingha. Most of the plays produced in the period were centered on a male protagonist. Women appeared in the plays as wives, mothers, girlfriends or mistresses; not many had an autonomous existence. Even some plays that seemingly provided a more balanced gender perspective ultimately succumbed to the workings of patriarchal ideology. For example, while *The Bearer of Woes* purports to present the perspectives of the Man and Woman, the play is structurally woven around the man's narrative. The man claims, "I'll tell you *our* story so you people can understand *my* position in all this." The play within the play is essentially the man telling "our story" with the intended goal of making people comprehend his position. The Woman is not given such a space. We witness how the actors and the director address the Man directly while the Woman gets systematically sidelined as the play progresses. Except for one actress in the troupe who sympathizes with the Woman, the others chastise her with a moral lens. The play gives a comprehensive view of the Man's dreams, while the audience remains unaware of the Woman's inner world and aspirations.

In the first ending of *The Jury*, Manuvansa returns from prison, having undergone a complete personality change, and directs his uncontrollable wrath at Sunvunā. As a devoted wife, she endures all his insults and physical violence. Initially in the play, she appears in the court scene to support Manuvansa; she then reappears at the end to get beaten up and abused by him. It is true that most of the characters in the play are based on certain stereotypes, but the fundamental issue with Sunvunā's character is that she has no other purpose but to support Manuvansa in the beginning of the play and then become the object of his physical abuse at the end. She seems but an afterthought.

Shadows and Men follows Dungura's trajectory in life; he meets Chukkina during his journey. In their initial meeting Dungura claims, "People say you are a bad woman and come up with evidence to prove it." This and the idea that she was "born in the streets" remain two very specific details in a play that otherwise is predominately abstract in its overall framework. What are the social implications of a bad woman in the streets? This factor is all the more baffling given that it does not contribute to the other themes in the play, except in the preceding scene where Chukkina claims that love is connected to lust while Dungura sees their meeting as a romantic encounter. Is the playwright unable to envisage a sexually autonomous woman without marking her as "a bad woman"? This specific detail perhaps speaks of a fundamental dis-ease in the way in which women's sexuality is explored in Sinhala theater.

A particular male fantasy reaches its height in *Aren't You Going to Shoot Me?* as the woman's legs—unseen by the spectator—stand for sexual desire, frustration and class aspirations. Apart from this pervasive presence of the fair legs, which quite interestingly signify a lack and an absence, and the fantasy sequence, women are otherwise absent in the play. Even in the fantasy scene, women's stereotypes abound as we meet Indira, the wife who constantly nags the husband about weddings, dresses and dentists. These plays were written several decades ago and some of the playwrights have moved onto explore gender and sexuality in complex ways, but since Sri Lankan Sinhala theater remains an essentially male domain, it is necessary to point out some of these issues related to gender politics that pervaded the plays written and performed in the 1980s and 1990s.[18]

Stage settings and other elements

The five plays in this collection capture the complexity of the times as well as the various modes that the dramatists were experimenting with in the 1980s and 1990s. Almost all of the plays move beyond realistic theatrical practices and integrate elements that break the illusion of a self-contained world on stage. *Goddess of Illusion* begins with a narrator who introduces a group of demons and gods to the audience and then moves to the setting of the modern-day funeral parlor. The narrator appears in multiple moments in the play to comment on the action, thus creating a critical distance between the performance and the audience while inviting them to pay attention to the various layers in the narrative. Karunarathne goes Brechtian in *The Jury* as the set transforms in front of the spectators: the pliable two boards, which indicate a wall in the beginning, are transformed into a table in the second scene. In a context where stage props readily available to be transformed into tables and walls, Hencharāla's demand for Manuvansa to kneel down and offer his back as a writing table makes a potent statement about the way in which the municipal worker is not given any respect as a human being. In terms of the stage settings, Rajitha Dissanayake's *Aren't You Going to Shoot Me?* might be the one that is the most realistic, but then he breaks the realism with the last fantasy sequence, which becomes all the more pronounced because it is rather banal. Jayakody's *Shadows and Men* weaves realistic elements with abstract and surreal elements; the small room and window are juxtaposed with the lone *pettagama*—a large box that is supposed to contain ancestral inheritance and valuable items—and the tall stick with a lantern hung on it. Abeysuriya's *The Bearer of Woes* breaks the fourth wall from the moment that the woman creates an unexpected commotion at the side entrance of the theater. *The Bearer of Woes*, which has plays within the play, also operates with a minimal use of stage props, a single door to be precise, which is propped up on a few occasions to indicate the entrance and exit to the woman's small shanty.

Another factor that I would like to mention is that all the playwrights in this volume are also the directors of the plays. Some of them are actors and directors of film and television dramas, while others work on production aspects of theater. Such engagement is common in the Sri Lankan theater context, and many a theater artist can navigate myriad areas in theater, as well as other visual and performing arts, with ease. At the same time, the plays that you find here were staged prior to their publication and the scripts were published after the performances. In fact, this is the first time that Dhananjaya Karunarathne's *Jury* and Prasanna Jayakody's *Shadows and Men* will appear in a published volume in any language.

About the translator

Professor Ranjini Obeyesekere is a prolific translator and has contributed immensely to introducing classical and twentieth and twenty-first-century Sinhala texts to English language readers. In 2017, she published a volume of translated poems, a selection of classical, folk and modern poetry from Sinhala to English and she is currently the editor of a project of translating the fourteenth-century Sinhala version of the Jataka stories into English. Some of her other translations include *Yashodhara, Wife of the Bodhisattva: Translations of the Sinhala Yashodharavatha and the Yasodharapadānā* (2009) and *Portraits of Buddhist Women: Stories from the Saddharmaratnāvaliya* (2001). She has also translated plays such as Federico Garcia Lorca's *The House of Bernarda Alba* and John Synge's *Riders to the Sea* into Sinhala. Her book *Sri Lankan Theatre in a Time of Terror* (1999) examines the politics of theater practice in Sri Lanka in the 1980s and 1990s, in the period known as the "time of terror." In short, Obeyesekere is firmly grounded in translation and theater and brings her versatile knowledge of both areas to this collection. She has spent several years translating and revising the texts. I admire her effort and perseverance in her aim to make Sinhala texts available in English for a wider readership.

Translating plays poses particular challenges to the translator because she has to imagine a number of semiotic systems that are not present on the page; she has to consider all the other significations that come into play outside of the linguistic text. The translator has to visualize the performance and think of the way in which language, which is only one component of the theatrical text, functions within a larger system.[19] Since Ranjini Obeyesekere has been actively engaged in theater as a director, translator and actor, it is with an awareness of the complexities in theater translation that she approaches these texts.[20] The five plays in this collection are different in tone, style and language. Obeyesekere has managed to capture these differences in her excellent translations. She has given them life in another language and hence in other spaces, times and realities.

Kanchuka Dharmasiri
University of Peradeniya, August 2020

Notes

1 *Abhinaya. Dramatists in the Seventies.* (Volume 9). Ed. Chandrasiri Bogamuwa. Battaramulla: Department of Cultural Affairs, 2003.
2 Dharwadker, Aparna. "Modern Indian Theatre." *Routledge Handbook of Asian Theatre.* Ed. Siyuan Liu. London: Routledge, 2016, 246.
3 The JVP (Janatha Vimukthi Peramuna/People's Liberation Front) is a political party that was founded in the mid-1960s. The JVP Identified itself as a Marxist revolutionary party and fought for economic and social rights of the rural youth. Their first armed insurrection in 1971 was a struggle against economic and political policies of the state. Yet, in the 1980s, it aligned with Sinhala nationalist forces in the South of the island and its second armed insurrection (from 1987 to 1989) was fought mainly against the Indo-Lanka accord signed between the Indian and Sri Lankan governments.
4 The JVP was banned in 1983 along with two other Leftist parties, namely Nava Sama Samaja Party (NSSP) and the Communist Party. Although the ban on the two latter parties were lifted in the same year, the JVP remained a banned party till 1994, which forced them to work underground.
5 Mudalāli is a term used for a businessman.
6 Abhinaya. *Dramatists in the Seventies.* (Volume 9). Ed. Chandrasiri Bogamuwa. Battaramulla: Department of Cultural Affairs, 2003, 388.
7 Haththotuwegama, Gamini. "Unresolved Contradictions, Paradoxical Discourses and Alternative Strategies in the Post-Colonial Sinhala Theatre" (1998). *Streets Ahead with Haththotuwegama.* Eds. Kanchuka Dharmasiri, Lohan Gunaweera and Nicole Calandra, Maharagama: Ravaya, 2012, 245.
8 Ediriweera Sarachchandra's introduction to K.B. Herath's *Maya Devi* (Kottawa: Sara Publishers and Printers, 1998), 16.
9 Bertolt Brecht. "Measures Taken." Trans. Carl R. Mueller. *Measures Taken and Other Lehrstucke* (London: Bloomsbury, 1977), 24.
10 Ranjini Obeyesekere. *Sri Lankan Theater in a Time of Terror.* (New Delhi: Sage Publications, 1999), 146.
11 In the dominant Theravada tradition in the country, it is held that only a man can achieve the status of Buddha, while women can only play supportive roles in that process.
12 The name Manuvansa literally means humankind. Most of the names in Karunarathne's play have such meanings. For example, Hencharāla means Henchman, Wahanse means a religious figure and Sunvuna means all over.
13 Bertolt Brecht, "The Exception and the Rule." Trans. Ralph Manheim. *Measures Taken and Other Lehrstucke,* 35.
14 A third ending to the play was written recently. It is included in the appendix. I am focusing on the first two endings here because we are speaking of the play in the context in which these endings were initially performed.

15 Ranjini Obeyesekere's footnote to the play.
16 Gamini Haththotuwegama. "Unresolved Contradictions, Paradoxical Discourses and Alternative Strategies in the Post-Colonial Sinhala theatre." *Streets Ahead with Haththotuwegama*. Eds. Kanchuka Dharmasiri, Lohan Gunaweera & Nicole Calandra, (Maharagama: Ravaya, 2012), 248.
17 Liyanage Amarakeerthi's introduction to Rajitha Dissanayake's *No Return*. Trans. Hasini Haputhanthri & Gihan de Chikera (Kandana: Winranga Publishers, 2013), 16.
18 I discuss this issue in "From Narratives of National Origin to Bloody Streets: Contemporary Sinhala and Tamil Theatre in Sri Lanka." *Mapping South Asia through Comtemporary Theatre*. Ed. Ashis Sengupta. (Palgrave Macmillan, 2014).
19 As Susan Bassnett notes, "the linguistic system is only one optional component in a set of interrelated systems that comprise the spectacle." Susan Bassnett, *Translation Studies*. London and New York: Routledge, 1980, 120.
20 During a conversation we had about the translation process, Obeyesekere claimed that she was not quite sure whether she was able to capture the visual elegance of a production such as Prasanna Jayakody's *Shadows and Men* in her translation. This particular example points out the type of challenges that a translator of plays encounters.

References

Abhinaya. *Dramatists in the Seventies*. (Volume 9). Ed. Chandrasiri Bogamuwa. Battaramulla: Department of Cultural Affairs, 2003

Bassnett, Susan. *Translation Studies*. London and New York: Routledge, 1980.

Brecht, Bertolt. *Measures Taken and Other Lehrstucke (Modern Plays)*. London: Bloomsbury, 1977.

Dharmasiri, Kanchuka. "From Narratives of National Origin to Bloody Streets: Contemporary Sinhala and Tamil Theatre in Sri Lanka". *Mapping South Asia Through Comtemporary Theatre*. Ed. Ashis Sengupta. Palgrave Macmillan, 2014

Dharwadker, Aparna. "Modern Indian Theatre." *Routledge Handbook of Asian Theatre*. Ed. Siyuan Liu. London: Routledge, 2016.

Dissanayake, Rajitha. *No Return*. Trans. Hasini Haputhanthri and Gihan de Chikera. Kandana: Winranga Publishers, 2013.

Haththotuwegama, Gamini. "Unresolved Contradictions, Paradoxical Discourses and Alternative Strategies in the Post-Colonial Sinhala Theatre" (1998). *Streets Ahead with Haththotuwegama*. Eds. Kanchuka Dharmasiri, Lohan Gunaweera & Nicole Calandra. Maharagama: Ravaya, 2012,

Herath, K.B. *Māyā Dēvi*. Kottawa: Sara Publishers and Printers, 1998.

Obeyesekere, Ranjini. *Sri Lankan Theatre in a Time of Terror*. New Delhi: Sage, 1999.

GODDESS OF ILLUSION (MĀYĀ DĒVI 1984)

K.B. Herath

The characters

All the characters in this play are connected by name with familiar Hindu gods. This divine or demonic association gives an added dimension and produce an ironic undercurrent to the developing plot.[1]

Briefly, in Hindu cosmology, Brahma is the creator of the world. Shiva is the destroyer. Shiva has two wives Kāli and Durga (fearsome.) Vishnu is the supporter of Existence with his wives Lakshmi or Sirikata (bestowing blessings and prosperity) and Sarastavti representing the arts. The last three are Rudra (a fierce and violent deity), Shani (the planetary deity Saturn who can bring misfortune for a 19-year period for those under its influence), and Yama (the god of death).

THE VISITOR/THE NARRATOR (Brahma)—A singer, who appears intermittently in the guise of a god.

MUDALĀLI[2] (Shiva)—The owner of the undertaking business/about 50 years of age

WIFE / CARALINA HAMI (Kali)—The-Mudalāli's wife/about 50 years of age

DOREGAMA HĀMINĒ (Durga)—The Mudalāli's sister/Sugath's mother/about 45 years of age

SUGATH (Vishnu)—A young man about 22 years old—Denagama Hāminē's son. Formerly a monk but encouraged to give up the robes and return to lay life.

LAKSHMI (Sirikatha)—The Mudalāli's elder daughter /a disabled young woman/ about 20 years old

SARASVATHI (Sarasvathi)—A young woman studying music/22 years old—Sugath's girlfriend

SAMSON (Rudra)—Mudalāli's son/28 years old

NEWTON (Shani)—The man who embalms in the undertaking business/35 years old

SIMON (Yama)—A funeral home broker for the sale of caskets; disabled as a result of electrocution/40 years old

Prologue

Ritual drums sound. The curtains open on a darkened stage. Shadowy forms can be seen on stage. The spot light center stage falls on the narrator's face. He sings in a slow rhythmic chant. As he chants the first two lines of the verse the left side of the stage lights up and the forms of the deities Sirikatha, Vishnu and Sarasvathi[3] *can be seen in a group. With the next two lines, the figures of Kali, Shiva and Durga*[4] *appear. With the second verse, the figures of Rudra, Shani and Yama*[5] *light up. With the final verse, the entire stage is lit up, after which the forms slowly fade out one by one.*[6]

The chant:

Oh, great god Vishnu! You who bear on your shoulders the goddess of prosperity, Siri, and the goddess of learning Sarasvathi, grace this earth!

Oh, merciful goddess Kali and mother-goddess Durga, you wives of god Shiva, grace this earth!

Ye gods who were crowned victors of the Kruta[7] *age, and you who adorned the Dvapara age bless us.*

The god Shani and Rudra, the prince of death, now bring the curse of the gods down on this earth!

Alas! The great king Mahā Sammata[8] *now ushers in the Kali-yug, that dark age that foreshadows the end of our world.*

The goddess of happiness, Siri, comes now in demonic form. Sarasvathi, the goddess of learning, bolts out the back door,

And heaven opens its gates to Vessamuni, the demon king.[9]

Act one

An undertaker's shop close to a hospital with a display of valuable coffins. Two elephant tusks[10] *and two traditional ceremonial banners (Sēsath) can be seen at the back, also a cross and a memorial tablet. The sign "Jonklass Undertakers" is hung at the front of the stage.*

The Mudalāli[11] *brings a wreath and places it up front on the stage. His wife enters from the back of the stage.*

WIFE: All the doctors say the same thing. I don't know what bad karma we must have accumulated to have to suffer like this. No other woman has gone through what I have! When will it end?

MUDALĀLI: Yes, what a pile of money we have spent on this illness! Every time you've come up with the name of a new doctor we've taken her to him.

We even tried the mental hospital. We've performed hundreds of exorcisms. In fact, we've had so many performed that now the girl knows all the ritual chants by heart! Such illnesses were unheard of in the time of our fathers and forefathers.

WIFE: I hear it is quite common in foreign lands. Some doctors seem to think it is all in her mind. I'm convinced the poor girl was scared out of her wits growing up in this coffin shop. How often I told you to sell this business and go in for something else. But when did you ever listen to anything I said!

MUDALĀLI: There is no other business in the whole wide world as lucrative as this, Hāminē.[12] One can make good profits with very little investment. Besides, it's the job I've been trained to do since I was a young man. These coffins are now almost a part of me. Anyway, the doctors never said that her illness was caused by the coffins.

WIFE: The doctors did say it was a mental illness—probably because she was born crippled. They also say that if we find her a husband there's a good chance she will recover fully.

MUDALĀLI: Doctors may say this and that, but how in the world are we going to find a husband for her? Who is going to marry her, however much dowry we offer? Will anyone with eyes in their head agree to such a marriage? She's crippled and blabbers like a loony. Besides, one can never tell when she'll have a fit. I ask you, who is the man that will agree to marry her?

WIFE: It's no use saying we can't find a man for her. We must find one. If her condition continues like this for two or three more months they say she might even kill herself.

MUDALĀLI: Just to get her married can we give her to any beggar off the street? He would have to be someone who fits our social status and way of life even minimally, especially since we still have the younger girl to marry off. Besides, the girl's horoscope says that any man she marries will die!

WIFE: Must we be concerned about the man she marries dying? Isn't it our daughter's life we should worry about? Besides, if this girl gets more and more crazy, how will we ever get the younger one married?

MUDALĀLI: What if everyone we ask refuses, in spite of the big dowry we offer? We can't do anything then.

WIFE: You only say you "can" if it has to do with corpses. Everything else you "can't do." Don't you think it might be a good idea to discuss this matter with Doregama Hāminē?

MUDALĀLI: What! With my sister? What can she do about it? She's done nothing but sigh and mourn since the day her man died. Besides, that man died only after he had buried them and their house under a load of debt.

WIFE: You may be a big businessman, but you don't have the brains of one of those corpses in your coffins!

MUDALĀLI: What?

WIFE: Yes, you may well say "What"! As if your sister doesn't have an only son—your nephew. What we have to do is see if we can marry the girl off to him.

MUDALĀLI: It's not just my daughter who is mad, I think the mother is going mad too! The only son my sister has is a monk and he's celibate! He took his higher ordination only the other day.

WIFE: That's just what I was about to say.

MUDALĀLI: What now? Are you suggesting I have the girl also ordained?

WIFE: Oh god! What a man! Just tell your sister that we need someone to run this business. Your sister is well aware that the only male child we have is a drunk and a ne'er-do-well. You tell her that if she can get her son to give up his monk's robes and come here, we will write over the undertaker's business to him.

MUDALĀLI: Oh, no, no! Certainly not! I will not write my undertaking business over to anyone. Not till I die.

WIFE: You don't have to actually write it. Just say you intend to do it, today, tomorrow, whenever; and keep postponing it till our job is done. Or else tell them you'll pay off the debt on their house.

MUDALĀLI: That's no easy task—paying off those debts of theirs.

WIFE: Is our child's life not more important than money? Besides, though you agree to give her the money to pay off her debt that doesn't mean you have to actually do it.

MUDALĀLI: All right. Let's say we promise him the money, and he agrees to give up his robes and come here. What then? What's to say he will want to marry the girl—being such a handsome young man himself!

WIFE: They say men who give up the celibate life are awfully greedy for women. When he finds the girl hanging around here it will all happen pretty quickly. He won't care about her being crazy. Once her sickness is cured then we can decide whether to go through with the deal or not.

MUDALĀLI: Say we promise him money, make him give up his robes and bring him here. What happens if the girl is not cured? We won't be able to chase him out at that point. What if we have to give him the money and the business?

WIFE: The doctor said she would be cured if she had a relationship with a man.

MUDALĀLI: My dear wife, do you know how many coffins I have sold to people whom the doctors said would be cured?

WIFE: That's not it. You love your money more than you love your own child. That's what it's all about.

MUDALĀLI: Even if I were to suggest this to my sister, do you think she'd agree? It was she who encouraged her son to become a monk. That young man is very bright and doing well in his studies. It is very unlikely that he'll come here.

WIFE: One can't earn five cents these days, either by becoming a monk or by doing well in one's studies. Didn't you hear that the young monk in our temple shed his robes last week and went abroad? They say he is making good money over there as a plumber. Besides, you know that if you promise your sister money, there is nothing you can't get her to do. When you promise to hand over such a flourishing business who is the monk who will refuse?

MUDALĀLI: Such deeds can land us in hell, wife.

WIFE: Isn't your daughter's life more important than your going to hell?

MUDALĀLI: No wonder they say that a woman can't think beyond the end of her cooking ladle. If we bring someone like that and marry him to our daughter what if he takes over everything? What will become of our other daughter? What will be left for our own son, Samson? He may be a drunk but must we leave him a beggar too?

WIFE: You sit there thinking about all those possibilities and what's going to happen to our daughter?

LAKSHMI: *(from within)*

Eighteen demon forms I'll take on
Eighteen demonic dreams I'll dream

WIFE: There, you hear her now. The manic fit has got worse again. I don't care whom we sacrifice but we must save this child.

LAKSHMI: *(enters singing)*

I will capture first-born maidens
I will roast Na-bloom-like babies.
I will call forth handsome princes …

WIFE: You see. Oh god! How can you sit there and do nothing?

MUDALĀLI: Lakshmi, Lakshmi, daughter.

LAKSHMI: Yes.

MUDALĀLI: I told you before my girl, you must not come here to the shop. How many times have I told you, wife, not to let the girl come in here? It makes her condition worse.

WIFE: Are you asking me to tie her to a tree? Come my child, let us go home.

LAKSHMI: I climbed on the back of this strange creature and flew to Singapore yesterday. We flew over, over the clouds, didn't we? Let's go to Japan today … But I warn you. If you go too slow, I'll twist your tail.

Oh … Oh … here's a coffin. There's another coffin.

(sings)

… Here a coffin, there a coffin,
Everywhere a coffin, coffin …

MUDALĀLI: For heaven's sake, take the girl home. If someone were to come now what will they think?

WIFE: Let's go home child. Come … come now. It was about you my child, that we were talking just now.

LAKSHMI: *Here a coffin, there a coffin, everywhere a coffin …*

WIFE: There you see. Her madness is much worse. This is not the time to be thinking of the rights and wrongs of an issue. I don't care who or what we sacrifice if we can only cure our child.

MUDALĀLI: I don't know what to do, wife.

WIFE: What don't you know? Just tell your sister when she next comes, that if she gets her son out of his robes and brings him here, that you will pay off all her debts. But don't talk of marriage just yet.

MUDALĀLI: I may make a living selling coffins Hāminē, but how can I, in cold blood, offer a man as a living sacrifice? What is more, a former monk!

WIFE: When push comes to shove, one has to throw the outsider to the dogs and save one's own. But that's not the problem. I know you. You always pull for your side of the family. You love your sister's son more than you love me or your own daughter.

MUDALĀLI: Woman[13], stop that talk. Don't make me mad or you'll hear an obscenity or two from me!

WIFE: Forget the obscenities. When your sister comes today talk this over with her and bring the boy here quickly. We'll see to the rest later …

MUDALĀLI: Ah, here comes Newton.

NEWTON: (*enters with a letter*) Mudalāli, the coffin we gave on credit to that playwright who died the other day has not been paid for yet. Here's another letter from the wife saying that things are very tight for her these days.

MUDALĀLI: When was it never tight for them? Hereafter, don't you give those good-for-nothing actors and theater people coffins on credit.

NEWTON: I see Simon running in this direction. Someone must have just died at the hospital.

MUDALĀLI: Does that raven of death come croaking? How many times has he said, "There's a patient in Ward 18 breathing his last; the businessman in Ward 32 has just died; there's yet another about to draw his last breath soon." But the corpses that come to me are here because of my ability, not because of him.

WIFE: I feel sorry for the man. He was well employed—until he happened to get electrocuted and barely survived.

MUDALĀLI: He may have suffered from the electrocution but the job he now has is far better than the one he had. Fifty bucks each time from the relatives of the dead man and 50 bucks from the undertaker! Not at all bad!

WIFE: But the man is half dead himself. He doesn't know at what moment he will collapse and die.

MUDALĀLI: You can't wait around trying to figure out when you are going to die. If you want to survive in these times you must find out when others are going to die.

LAKSHMI: (*singing from within the house*)

He lives within the stumpy stump beside the Sidda ford,
And all the creatures of the fields his divine eye beholds.

MUDALĀLI: Looks as if she's about to get her attack again. Go stop her before she starts running down the road.

Wife leaves.

SIMON: (*Enters. He has constant tremors as he has suffered a severe electric shock.*) Mudalāli, the man in Ward No.13 is breathing his last.

MUDALĀLI: Breathing his last? Are you sure?

SIMON: I'm quite sure. Do I lie? I've been peeping into his room for the past hour now.

MUDALĀLI: Yes, but will he actually die?

SIMON: I'm telling you, have a coffin ready in ten minutes.

MUDALĀLI: So soon? Is he a rich man?

SIMON: He is a veritable money-tree. He's a businessman, a Mudalāli.

MUDALĀLI: About how much should we charge for the coffin?

SIMON: Well over five thousand rupees for sure. However, if you want the body, I must have my commission now.

MUDALĀLI: Commission? How can I pay a commission like that? What if the man doesn't die?

SIMON: Well, if you can't pay the commission the body goes to the undertaker down the road.

MUDALĀLI: That rogue down the road?

SIMON: Yes.

MUDALĀLI: Well ...well ... (*taking the money out of his purse*) you're sure he'll die?

SIMON: What nonsense you talk. Do you think people call me Death-Demon-Saima[14] for nothing? Have the coffin ready. I'm off.

MUDALĀLI: Newton! Newton!

NEWTON: Yes Mudalāli.

MUDALĀLI: Get a No. 3 coffin and the hearse ready.

NEWTON: I was about to tell you, sir, we are out of formalin for embalming and there's no diesel for the hearse.

MUDALĀLI: What? Have you taken to drinking the formalin and the diesel?

NEWTON: It's not me. The young master took the hearse yesterday and went off on a trip with some young women. That is how the diesel was finished.

MUDALĀLI: The young master?

NEWTON: Yes.

MUDALĀLI: I've told him not to step into this shop. Why did you allow him to take the hearse? Oh, if only I had a son with brains, I would be the richest man in the land today. Instead, what do I have? Not as if I didn't send him to one of the best colleges for his education. All he did was hang around with the dropouts. Didn't learn a thing. Now he's ended up an alcoholic and sells my coffins from my shop to find the money for his drinking and gambling. Don't let him come near this place again, you hear. Hm ... Well go now and buy some more formalin and diesel. Buy the diesel from the shed at the corner and the formalin from the fish shop owner.[15]

SAMSON: (*singing outside*)

NEWTON: There comes the young master again!

MUDALĀLI: Let him come. I'll teach him a lesson!

SAMSON: (*enters singing*) Papa![16]

MUDALĀLI: Papa! Haven't I told you not to put your foot inside this coffin shop? Going on jaunts and shamelessly running around with young women in a hearse!

SAMSON: If it's good enough to take corpses in, what's wrong with taking some girls in it?

MUDALĀLI: Good enough to take corpses! I've told you not to step in here.

SAMSON: If you did what I told you to do, I wouldn't have to come here.

MUDALĀLI: What is it you want me to do?

SAMSON: If you wrote this undertaking business over to me today, tomorrow I could mortgage it and get a loan for five or six million. Thereafter we'll import coffins from Japan. They're not like these useless wooden boxes. They're fully aluminum. There is a spring board under where you keep the corpse. The moment you press a switch the whole bed rises with the corpse. You have no idea, Papa, what it takes to do business these days. With the Japanese coffins if you sell one a month it will be more than enough. From just one sale you'll make about a hundred-thousand-rupee profit.

MUDALĀLI: When you couldn't make a profit selling the coffins that we already have here, how will you do it with coffins bought from abroad?

SAMSON: That's not for you to worry about, Papa. All I need in order to get a loan is the title to the business.

MUDALĀLI: I will never write this undertaking firm over to anyone. Not till I die. Besides, I'm thinking of taking in a man to help run this business.

SAMSON: Taking in a man? A rank outsider?

MUDALĀLI: Well, not quite. A relative.

SAMSON: Then you refuse to write the business to me?

MUDALĀLI: I've already told you so once, Samson.

SAMSON: OK, Papa. Just remember several people around here will be sleeping in these coffins before too long. Keep that in mind. Just save one for yourself!

He turns to leave.

MUDALĀLI: What was it you just said? You …

WIFE: (*entering*) What? Are father and son trying to kill each other now?

MUDALĀLI: The fellow thinks he can threaten me.

WIFE: (*shouting!*) I see your sister coming. The moment she arrives talk over what we discussed. See if you can get her to persuade her boy to give up his monk's robes. But tell her it is something you are keeping secret from me. I'll stay in the house till you finish your talk.

MUDALĀLI: I don't know what to do wife … When we bring an outsider in here who knows what Samson will do? I can't possibly mention this matter to him.

But I can't not mention it either. I'm convinced there'll be a killing here. He's not one to respect his parents' words.

WIFE: Now, don't arouse the devil in me. Do as I tell you. I will tackle Samson.

Doregama Hāminē enters.

DOREGAMA HĀMINĒ: Ah brother! Why was Samson shouting abuse at you as he walked out just now?

MUDALĀLI: Well, now you see, don't you? What's happened to me is far worse than what has happened to you. My son is a drunk and a madman. My older daughter is also not too well. Do sit down.

DOREGAMA HĀMINĒ: (*sitting*) That's the way of the world. It is the Kali-yug, brother. You can see the fate that has befallen me. All my man ever did while he was alive was to play music and loaf around singing. He got my only son ordained a monk. Ultimately, he left me to cope with a huge load of debt all alone …

MUDALĀLI: In fact, that's just what I wanted to talk to you about, sister … You know the situation with my son. The fellow is an alcoholic. I have reached the age when I no longer have the energy to manage all this alone. On the other hand, how can one close down a flourishing business such as this?

DORAGAMA HĀMINĒ: That's so, for sure. The only thing to do now is find a husband for the second girl and bring him into the family. The older girl, of course is likely to be an invalid all her life.

MUDALĀLI: I can't very well stop my younger girl's education. She's doing very well at her studies. By the way, how is our young monk these days?

DOREGAMA HĀMINĒ: You should just see him now! He's a great student. Excellent at his books! His sermons are way over the heads of ordinary mortals like us!

MUDALĀLI: Though he's like that now … who can tell? One of these days he might give up his robes and take up with some trashy floosy who'll hang herself around his neck.

DOREGAMA HĀMINĒ: Oh no! … Not even in a dream can such a thing ever happen! He's a very moral monk. Always walks with his eyes fixed on the ground.

MUDALĀLI. I've been thinking … had that young fellow not become a monk I could have handed over this business and property to him. My Hāminē's relatives are desperate to get a hold of it, but I have no love for that clan!

DOREGAMA HĀMINĒ: Property?

MUDALĀLI: Yes.

DOREGAMA HĀMINĒ: But if you can marry off your younger daughter the matter will be settled.

MUDALĀLI: That young girl is completely absorbed in her studies. She refuses to even think about such matters. Besides, even if she were to marry, an outsider is always an outsider. It's not like blood ties … What I would like, as I grow old, is some young man of my own blood to take over from me … Hm … I suppose your son has no thought of giving up the monkhood?

DOREGAMA HĀMINĒ: Oh no!

MUDALĀLI: That's it. How could he give it up just like that? But now … if you were to ask him sister, perhaps …

DOREGAMA HĀMINĒ: If I were to ask him?

MUDALĀLI: Yes.

DOREGAMA HĀMINĒ: But brother, how can I? I, who observe the eight precepts[17] every week, with every change of the moon, how can I even open my mouth to suggest such a thing?

MUDALĀLI: That's not the point. If your son gives up his monk's robes and comes here this property will all be his one day.

DOREGAMA HĀMINĒ: This property?

MUDALĀLI: Yes.

DOREGAMA HĀMINĒ: Then what about the children of this house?

MUDALĀLI: My son is a drunkard. My elder daughter is an invalid. And as for the younger girl, apart from her books she has no interest in anything.

DOREGAMA HĀMINĒ: I don't know what to say. These properties don't mean much to us. But … if it's going to be of some help to you brother … then again, how can I broach it to our young monk?

MUDALĀLI: Tell him the real story. Now that our young monk's father is dead you have no income to live on, have you? Your house and lands are mortgaged. If your son gives up his robes and does a job it would be to support his mother. That Act of Merit alone should be enough to send the man to nirvana! They say even the Bodhisattva carried his mother on his back and swam to safety … If you can get the boy to give up his robes and be with me in my old age, I, in turn, will pay up the mortgage on your house and lands.

DOREGAMA HĀMINĒ: You'll pay the mortgage?

MUDALĀLI: Yes. What do you say to that, sister?

DOREGAMA HĀMINĒ: But what will people say?

MUDALĀLI: People are not the ones who will give you food and shelter. Besides, don't imagine this is a trifling piece of luck to be ignored. What other man would do such a thing?

DOREGAMA HĀMINĒ: But how can I suggest something like this and then ever hope to step into that temple again, even to observe the precepts?

MUDALĀLI: Why must you go to that particular temple? There are enough other temples to which you can go. Where you observe the precepts, like where you buy a coffin, makes not the slightest difference!

DOREGAMA HĀMINĒ: But will our young monk do it just because I ask him to? The senior monk may give him a good scolding for even suggesting it.

MUDALĀLI: I don't know about all that. I'm merely trying to help you, sister, because of our blood ties. But if you can't persuade him then what's to be done?

DOREGAMA HĀMINĒ: To tell you the truth brother, I have been worried sick these past months, trying to think how I could pay off the mortgage on my house. It's no small sum.

MUDALĀLI: That's just what I said.

DOREGAMA HĀMINĒ: But how can I bring myself to do this?

MUDALĀLI: Well, if you really can't, then it's no matter. But it's a shame. This is a property worth several hundred thousands!

The sound of chanting is heard coming from the back.

MRS. DORAGAMA: Tomorrow, when I take the food offerings to the temple, I'll talk to our young monk and see. But I'm a woman who observes the precepts. I'm not too happy about doing this.

MUDALĀLI: That's good enough. Go in now to the house. But don't tell Caralina anything about this talk of property. Ah wife, here's my sister come to visit.

The stage goes dark.

THE NARRATOR:

With golden crown and blue silk shawl and ornaments divine,
Bow and arrows finely wrought, in powerful hands clasped tight,
With bands of gold and shawls divine and jewels of bird design
Great god Vishnu astride his mount the Gurula bird, arrives.

Act two

The undertaker's shop. Doregama Hāminē is seated there. Her son, Sugath, is standing beside her.

DOREGAMA HĀMINĒ: That's why I'm asking you to stay here.

SUGATH: Ugh! I can't bear to live here, Mother. It's so different from living in the monastery. This is all so strange to me.

DOREGAMA HĀMINĒ: Just think it over a bit, son. You know our house and property are all mortgaged.[18] I knew of the loan only after your father died. We must have some way to live. In this house, my brother's son is a drunkard. His elder daughter is crazy. Now the younger daughter is … she is your cross cousin and so you will be the first choice when it comes to marriage.

SUGATH: What are you saying, Mother!

DOREGAMA HĀMINĒ: What I'm saying, son, is that someday this million-rupee business will be ours. Thank god you can then live like a king! With this kind of money, I, too, can take to the religious life, observe the precepts, and live quietly without a care in the world.

SUGATH: But, Mother, I'm terrified to stay here amidst all these coffins.

DOREGAMA HĀMINĒ: Why should you be frightened? As a monk you must have been taught to meditate on death and decay and contemplate corpses?

SUGATH: When one meditates, the corpses are only in one's head. But here one sees corpses in flesh and blood!

DOREGAMA HĀMINĒ: With time, you'll learn to live even with a corpse child!

SUGATH: I can't. I really can't. I'll give up my robes and come home Mother, but I'll take on some other job.

DOREGAMA HĀMINĒ: What job will you do when you come home to our village? You have no land to farm. The house and property are all mortgaged. Your father died only after he had lost everything.

SUGATH: But I like to live in our village.

DOREGAMA HĀMINĒ: Live in the village?

SUGATH: Yes.

DOREGAMA HĀMINĒ: Oh yes! I know why you are so eager to live in the village!

SUGATH: Why? What is it?

DOREGAMA HĀMINĒ: What is it? Just because I hide the dirt in the dish by covering it with a lid,[19] don't imagine I'm a stupid cow. I heard the women at the temple gossiping. You won't be able to get away with that—not with this mother!

SUGATH: What are you talking about, Mother?

DOREGAMA HĀMINĒ: What? What is this affair you have with that woman Sarasvathi—that pauper?

SUGATH: Sarasvathi! You are mad, Mother. Sarasvathi only comes to teach at the Sunday school at the temple.

DOREGAMA HĀMINĒ: What can that creature teach? She's a woman who hangs out all day in the town!

SUGATH: She only goes to town to study music and dancing. Mother, you don't know how well Sarasvathi dances.

DOREGAMA HĀMINĒ: That's for sure! Dance she does! That's what she's learned to do throughout the length and breadth of the seven provinces—the cheap, traveling vagrant!

SUGATH: Mother, don't badmouth innocent people. Don't you remember how, when we were small, both Sarasvathi and I learned music from Father? We have been good friends since that time.

DOREGAMA HĀMINĒ: However that may be, her family is not good enough for us. Let's not discuss this anymore. Now, if you use your head and do as I tell you, you can be as rich as a king. You don't know the kind of a mother you have. If I went to all these lengths to persuade you to give up your robes, I'm no dumb buffalo, my son!

SUGATH: Whatever you may say, I just can't do it, Mother. I have no experience with this sort of thing.

DOREGAMA HĀMINĒ: Now, don't rouse the devil in me! Here's a business worth millions about to fall in your lap and you want to be like that luckless Pinguttara who sent his wife Udumbara up the fig tree![20]

SUGATH: The moment you leave I'm going back home too. This is like living in a cemetery.

DOREGAMA HĀMINĒ: Son, all my life I've never known anything called happiness. Your father had no head for business and no value for money. He was a playboy. If you leave, and throw away this good fortune that has come your way, I will die in a ditch, homeless, in these last years of my life.

MUDALĀLI: (*entering*) Now you, young man, must work here and think of this as your home.

DOREGAMA HĀMINĒ: That's just what I was saying too, brother.

MUDALĀLI: Let's see, you are …?

SUGATH: The Reverend Dorenegama Jinarathana Thera… but I'm now Sugath.

DOREGAMA HĀMINĒ: My son's future is now in your hands, brother. I must be going.

MUDALĀLI: Good. On your way out just step in and see my wife too.

DOREGAMA HĀMINĒ: Yes, I'll see Caralina. Son, I'll be leaving now.

SUGATH: Mother. (*He bows to her and bids goodbye.*)

DOREGAMA HĀMINĒ: The blessings of the Triple Gem be with you.[21] Hm … that's funny, before, it was I who bent down to worship you … (*She leaves.*)

MUDALĀLI: Now my young man, you must get used to the work here. It's very different from being a monk! If you want to make it in the world this is the best business to be in. The more men die the better for us. You don't know, my boy, how much I have prospered. Sit down, I'll tell you. I first came here as a hired hand.

SUGATH: A hired hand?

MUDALĀLI: Oh yes. This undertaker's shop was first begun by a white man named Jonklass. Though he was white, he was a gem of a man. He never married. He had suffered from a broken heart over some woman, so after a while he didn't care if he sold coffins or not. All he did was to get drunk on whiskey each evening and sing and dance. Like this …

You are my sunshine
My only sunshine
You make me happy
When skies are grey …

When I first came to work for him I was a young buck like you. My name was Vastuhāmi but the white man called me Westham. At first, I just did the fetching and carrying. Then I did the embalming. After that I became manager. After I married, the man became almost a member of the family. When he was about to leave for England he said to me "Westham, you are a good fellow. I will write this business to you."

SUGATH: I thought this was your very own business, Uncle.

MUDALĀLI: Of course, it is mine now. You should see how much I have developed the business. During the malaria epidemic there were days when I sold over a hundred coffins. Ah! when will a time like that ever come again! Now, my boy, you must learn to manage this business.

SUGATH: I don't understand anything about business, Uncle.

MUDALĀLI: There isn't very much to learn here. When you get up in the morning, all you have to do is light the lamp to the gods, place some incense sticks in front of the Sivali good luck image and wait for something to happen. If you don't begin with those rituals, the coffin sales drop.

SUGATH: Then, how do you price these coffins?

MUDALĀLI: It is not we who price the coffins, my boy. It's the people who come to buy them that do so. As they walk in the door you must figure out if they are moneyed folk or not. Now, if it's a school teacher or some clerk in an office, you won't get more than a thousand rupees. But if a business man dies, that's another matter. Unfortunately, businessmen don't seem to die in a hurry!

SUGATH: What are the cheapest coffins made of?

MUDALĀLI: They are made of Rukkatthana, that cheap wood.

SUGATH: What about those seven thousand rupee coffins?

MUDALĀLI: Oh, those, too, are of Rukkatthana.

SUGATH: Then what about the fifteen thousand rupee one?

MUDALĀLI: That's Rukkatthana too, man. They are all Rukkatthana. You had better just watch how I work for the first week or two. You'll soon learn. All you have to do is sell the coffins.

Newton enters.

MUDALĀLI: What time is it now?

NEWTON: A sad thing has happened, Mudalāli. The monk in our temple has just died.

MUDALĀLI: What? Just now!

NEWTON: No, a little while ago. They will be coming here soon.

MUDALĀLI: Quick, put a cushion into that coffin. Make it a yellow[22] one. Quick, quick. So, the old chief priest is gone! Look here … if I don't happen to be around, this young man will see to the work. Hm … hurry up. Go on now.

To Sugath

That was Newton, the driver of our hearse. There's one other thing. My son, Samson, may drop in wanting money. Just don't give him a penny.

WIFE: (*enters*) Don't confuse that poor boy with too much. Some flowers have just come in. Go and take charge of that.

SUGATH: (*leaves*)

WIFE: Now, if you stick around in here the whole day, all we've done so far will be of no use. If the girl has the place free to hang around in, they'll have a chance to meet and get to know each other. If you insist on sticking around, what we're hoping for won't happen.

MUDALĀLI: But that boy has just come. You can't expect all that to happen the moment he arrives.

WIFE: You may know a thing or two about dead men, but you don't know one puff ball about what live men do or think! There's no time to look for auspicious moments. The girl's illness is getting worse.

MUDALĀLI: So, then, what should we do?

WIFE: If you didn't plant yourself here but looked after things that have to be done outside, it would help.

MUDALĀLI: What if the organizers making arrangements for the funeral of the monk arrive?

WIFE: Yes, the only important thing in your life is the sale of a coffin! Even if there's a death in the family, you'll be inside here glued to a coffin!

MUDALĀLI: I know, I'm the scapegoat for everything. Look, I'm leaving now. You, wife, can dance whatever jig you want.

WIFE: Dance a jig! Yes, this is a game to you—a game—remember you are playing with the life of a human being.

Sugath enters reading a book. He sits by a table.

WIFE: Did you count the flowers before taking them?

SUGATH: Yes.

WIFE: What I was about to tell you my son, is that, after all, we are not outsiders. The Mudalāli is your very own uncle. I'm your aunt. Then … this place should be like your home. What is it that you have there?

SUGATH: I'm trying to do a little studying. There's no harm in that, is there? I've signed up to take the exam this year.

WIFE: You don't have to bury yourself in your books now that you are here. It's not like when you were at the monastery. I'll ask my daughter to drop by for a little chat.

SUGATH: No, that's not necessary, Aunt.

WIFE: But you must be so bored and lonely here, my child.

SUGATH: No, I'm not lonely, Aunt.

WIFE: Lakshmi has given me no peace. She wants to meet you. I will ask her to come.

SUGATH: (*as she is leaving*) But Aunt …

(*he reads*) *yada balaka suchipanna rachchda—kalassa mesassa …*[23]

NEWTON: (*enters*) Hey there! Where's the Mudalāli?

SUGATH: Why? Is it a coffin you want? I'm sorry I thought you had come to buy a coffin.

NEWTON: Then you are now the boss here?

SUGATH: I don't know …

NEWTON: Oh, but we know you. You used to be a monk once, weren't you?

SUGATH: Who said so?

NEWTON: There's no need to get excited. What's wrong with having once been a monk? However, remember this now. When the Mudalāli quotes five thousand for a coffin, you sir, must quote it as seven thousand.

SUGATH: Then?

NEWTON: Well then, you and I sir, will share the two thousand.

SUGATH: Ugh! That would be stealing. It's a sin.

NEWTON: Steal! Who is stealing? Sir, don't you use those dirty words here in this coffin shop. We are not stealing. We are engaging in business. We are only making a commission. Now, the biggest commissions come when the coffins we have sold come back.

SUGATH: The coffins you sell come back? What do you mean?

NEWTON: You know how this business works, sir. Now let's say we sold a very good coffin. It comes back to the shop that night.

SUGATH: (*alarmed*) What?

NEWTON: Don't be alarmed. It comes back without the corpse. You see this coffin over here that's eighteen thousand rupees. It has been sold over ten times already.

SUGATH: Oh god!

NEWTON: Sir, why be scared? One small shot to drink and you'll get over it.

SUGATH: Ugh! I don't drink that muck.

NEWTON: Sir, you seem fit only to be a monk! A small shot … and … you surely must have some women friends …

SUGATH: What women friends?

NEWTON: Let's meet later and talk. I must go now. I have a small job to do.

SUGATH: (*stopping Newton as he is about to leave*) I hear there is a music class somewhere in town. Do you know where that is?

NEWTON: Why do you ask that, sir? You came here to sell coffins not to make music.

SUGATH: No, I just wanted to find out where the place was.

NEWTON: What for? Ah … I understand … right, right. Ha! Ha! I understand now. It's in the center of town, sir. There are some great girls there. (*He is about to leave again.*)

SUGATH: It's not the girls, man. I want to learn a little music.

NEWTON: Can you play an instrument, sir?

SUGATH: Yes. From the time we were children we studied music. Didn't you know our father—he was called Gītasinghe, the Lion of Song—he was a very famous musician.[24]

NEWTON: Yes, yes. But what I meant to say was—a music class has many uses. I have to go now to sew a cushion in a coffin. We'll organize a great party soon.

He leaves. Sugath sits and reads his book. Lakshmi enters from the back, peeps through the door and throws her toy animal Ayra at him. Sugath gets up frightened.

LAKSHMI: Ha! Ha! Haa! Sadhu![25] Your worship!

SUGATH: Sadhu? What sadhu! I'm Sugath.

LAKSHMI: But you are a sadhu, a monk.

SUGATH: What's that you have in your hand? A horse?

LAKSHMI: Ayra is not a horse. That's my Ayra.

SUGATH: What?

LAKSHMI: There, do you see him in that picture, standing there in the middle.
SUGATH: But that's the god Vishnu.
LAKSHMI: You are Vishnu.
SUGATH: Good god, what are you saying!

The stage darkens. Lakshmi and Sugath are on stage looking on. From the back, standing as if in the iconic postures of gods and goddesses are the Mudalāli, his wife, Doregama Hāminē, Saraswati, Samson and Simon. They sing.

Reigning over the open sky
Are the gods of the universe
Nestling in the lap of the earth
human denizens.

Let's become gods of the universe
We humans who walk the earth
In this same world we are gods
—we are humans
In a single instant we are gods
—we are humans
One moment—gods
One moment—humans.

But the gods who won the hearts of humans
Flew away with the goddess Sirikatha
The humans who hid in heaven above
Became the demons of the Kali-yug.

The images fade and disappear. The stage lights up.

LAKSHMI: There he is as big as life. That's Ishwara—my father. The one at the side—that's Kali—my mother. That scowling one—that's Durga—your mother. That one who is laughing—that's Rudra—my brother. That one like a demon—that's Death-Demon-Saima.
SUGATH: Who told you all that?
LAKSHMI: It was in a book—in the god's temple.
SUGATH: But this is not a temple of the gods. This is a coffin shop.
LAKSHMI: Yes, these are coffins. All the corpses inside are cripples.[26] (*tauntingly*) Hoo! … Hoo ! You are a cripple too!
SUGATH: I?
LAKSHMI: (*chants*)

She shook her fiery anklet
She torched King Pandi's town
then came here.[27]

SUGATH: What's that supposed to mean?

LAKSHMI: You are very mean. When we were children and used to play together and you were always taunting me.

SUGATH: I? What did I say?

LAKSHMI: You called me a cripple. (*hesitatingly*) Mother said … Mother told me ….

SUGATH: What did your mother say?

LAKSHMI: Mother said you had asked me to come here just now. You did ask me to come? Didn't you?

SUGATH: What? Ah yes, yes! I did.

LAKSHMI: Shall I tell you a lovely story?

SUGATH: Lakshmi, please leave. I have work to do.

LAKSHMI: No, no. Once upon a time there was a beautiful princess.

SUGATH: Yes, and that princess had a lame leg!

LAKSHMI: What did you say? … Have you ever seen brides?

SUGATH: Brides?

LAKSHMI: Yes. I've collected all the pictures of brides that appear in the newspapers.

SUGATH: Why did you do that?

LAKSHMI: Then you can choose a good one from among them. Wait a moment. I'll get them.

SUGATH: No, no, no. I don't want them.

LAKSHMI: No. I'll get them for you.

She leaves. Sarasvathi enters from the other side.

SARASVATHI: Hey! Sugath!

SUGATH: Sarasvathi! What are you doing here?

SARASVATHI: I came for my music class. I go by here every day. Our music classes are held in that building over there. You can see it from here.

SUGATH: Is that so? In fact, I asked several people where the music classes were being held.

SARASVATHI: When you said you were coming to work in a shop I didn't for a moment dream it would be a coffin shop! Ugh! How can you stay here Sugath?

SUGATH: I'm not here because I like it. But Mother wouldn't leave me in peace until I came.

SARASVATHI: Your mother is a very tough lady, isn't she?

SUGATH: Why? Did she say anything to you?

SARASVATHI: No, nothing. But whenever she sees me she scowls at me like a Kali.

SUGATH: I won't stay here long, Sarasvathi.

SARASVATHI: When I see these coffins, I keep remembering my dead brother. We couldn't afford one for him. To me, these coffins seem to sit on piles and piles of money.

SUGATH: I was asked to attend your brother's funeral. But I did not come. We grew up together as children. I couldn't bear to look at his corpse. That's why I didn't come.

SARASVATHI: If my brother had remained in this country how many more years he might have lived.

SUGATH: What a superb actor he was. There are not many like him left.

SARASVATHI: But as an actor my brother could not earn enough to live on. My mother and all her friends began to yell at him to get a decent job. That's why he went abroad. He didn't really want to go.

SUGATH: He was gone barely a month.

SARASVATHI: Just 20 days … (*pause*) It took about 20 days to get the body down. He came in a box, wrapped in foil, on a bed of ice and sawdust … Since that day coffins disgust me, so does money!

SUGATH: But one has to live, Sarasvathi.

SARASVATHI: Why does one need so much money to live? I'm taking my finals in music this term. I may be able to find a teaching position. You can also join our class now.

SUGATH: If I go to music classes who will sell these coffins? Besides, I've almost forgotten all the music I knew.

SARASVATHI: You used to play the violin so well in those days. Do you remember how your father taught us both the violin? I could never play as well as you. Where is your violin?

SUGATH: It's at home. What use is a violin in this coffin shop? (*taking Sarasvathi's violin in his hand*) Did you buy this recently? I haven't touched a violin in a long time now.

He plays the Jayamangala Gatha[28] *(Stanzas of Victory) and begins to sing.*

Creating a thousand hands, with weapons armed.

Lakshmi enters with a bundle of newspapers in her hands.

LAKSHMI: (*chanting the second line of the Stanza*) Death-god Mara on the elephant Girimekala charged …

SARASVATHI: Mara? Who is that person?

SUGATH: That's my uncle's daughter. Don't talk to her. She's a loony.

SARASVATHI: How can you not go crazy living among these coffins!

LAKSHMI: Have you come to buy a coffin?

SARASVATHI: Er … Yes, yes.

LAKSHMI: Sakra, great Brahma, I greet you! …

SARASVATHI: This is a bloody mad-house—in addition to being a coffin shop!

LAKSHMI: Cousin Sugath asked me to find him a bride. Here, I've brought one.

SUGATH: I said no such thing. She's mad.

LAKSHMI: There's a whole pile of brides here. You can choose whoever you want.

SUGATH: I don't want any. Go home, Lakshmi.

LAKSHMI: (*picking up the violin case*) Why, what a lovely coffin you have here. How beautiful! Where's the corpse that was in it?

SARASVATHI: Corpse? Why there it is!

LAKSHMI: Hooo! This one has lost both legs!

SARASVATHI: Give that. (*tries to snatch her violin back*)

LAKSHMI: Grrr …! Come away. Come stand by my side, cousin.

SARASVATHI: Sugath, if you stay here you will surely be possessed by a demon. You can see that, can't you?

LAKSHMI: (*scowls at her*)

WIFE: (*entering*) Ah, you are here … Who is this?

SUGATH: She … she … is …

LAKSHMI: She has been singing the Victory Stanzas with cousin Sugath.

SARASVATHI: (*hurriedly*) I came to buy some flowers.

WIFE: Well, the flowers are in the back room. Go get them, Sugath, go get them for her.

Sugath leaves.

WIFE: This child acts crazy because of her fevered state.

SARASVATHI: She certainly acts crazy.

SUGATH: (*enters bringing her the flowers*) Here.

SARASVATHI: No, these are not the kind I wanted. (*She leaves.*)

WIFE: I didn't like the way that woman walked in here. She certainly didn't come to buy flowers. (*to Sugath*) This girl of mine gives me no peace. She insists she must come and talk to cousin Sugath. After all, you played together as children.

SUGATH: But Aunt, she seems to be quite mad now.

WIFE: No, it's just the high fever she's had that's causing it … It will go away in a day or two … Cousin Sugath must be feeling dull so you stay here with him, child. I must go now.

SUGATH: But Aunt …

He leaves the room with the flowers. Lakshmi picks up the book Sugath was reading and which is lying on stage. She reads a little and then begins to tear the pages. Sugath comes in and snatches the book from her.

LAKSHMI: (*chants*)

Oh demon Huniyan come with your flock
I'll cut its neck and offer you a cock.
come, full of greed, and bring us good luck
for a sacrificial offering take this cock.

She throws something at Sugath.

SUGATH: Oh god! Get out of here! This is a house of the damned! Go home.

Lakshmi dances, whirling round and round as in exorcisms and collapses in a trance.

WIFE: (*running in*) Lakshmi … Lakshmi … What did you say to the poor girl?

SUGATH: I didn't say anything.

WIFE: Lakshmi … Lakshmi.

LAKSHMI: (*slowly coming out of her trance*) Yes?

WIFE: Let's go home, my child.

She puts her arms around her and leads her out while Sugath looks on, terrified.

DEATH-DEMON-SAIMA: (*enters*) Huh!
SUGATH: Huh! ... Who are you?
SAIMA: I'm Death-Demon Saima ... Let's go.
SUGATH: Where to?
SAIMA: Anywhere. To there. To the hospital.
SUGATH: To hospital? Whatever for?
SAIMA: For a corpse. It is breathing its last. I want 50 bucks.
SUGATH: A man is breathing his last? Why should I give you 50 rupees just because a man is dying?
SAIMA: What the hell do you know! Where's the Mudalāli ... Mudalāli ... Mudalāli ...
NEWTON: (*enters*) Ah Saima. Have you brought us the goods?
SAIMA: There is one. I want 50.
NEWTON: The Mudalāli is not in. Bring the body. We'll pay.
SAIMA: I'll bring it. But you, Mr. Driver, must guarantee payment.
NEWTON: OK, OK.

Saima leaves.

SUGATH: What was that all about?
NEWTON: That was the broker for the dead. We give him 50 on each coffin.
SUGATH: Is that so?

Sounds of singing. Samson enters.

SUGATH: Cousin Samson!
SAMSON: Ho! You renegade monk! So, you are this big shot ... relative!

He sits on the table and opens a drawer.

SUGATH: Cousin Samson, Uncle told me not to give you any money when you ask for it.
SAMSON: Who the hell asked for it? There's nothing to ask. I just take it.
SUGATH: Please don't do that cousin Samson. Uncle will think I stole it.
SAMSON: So that's right. There was money in the drawer. Now it's gone. You are the thief.
SUGATH: Please cousin. I just can't allow you to take that money.
SAMSON: Who the hell are you to say that to me?
SUGATH: But Uncle Mudalāli has told me ...
SAMSON: So, it's Uncle Mudalāli now is it? Well, long before he became your uncle he was my father!
SUGATH: But cousin, I was asked to be responsible for the money.
SAMSON: Responsible! (*He pushes Sugath away and Sugath falls.*) What you're responsible for is to go back there to the monastery! Go back to your monastery. Go! No, don't bother. I'm going to start a coffin shop myself. I'll invite you, monk, to give the funeral sermons! (*He leaves.*)

NEWTON: (*returning*) I knew he was going to create trouble. But what's to be done. They've just brought in a fresh corpse. Let's go supervise the embalming of it.

SUGATH: No. I can't bear to watch that.

NEWTON: Come on. How can you do this business if you're that squeamish.

SUGATH: I can't. I'm afraid.

NEWTON: Come on. It's the corpse of a young woman who went abroad—a pretty girl.

They leave. The Mudalāli and his wife enter.

WIFE: I was wondering where you'd gone.

MUDALĀLI: Did they bring a body just now?

WIFE: Yes.

MUDALĀLI: That's it! Wherever I am, when they bring in a body I can sense it, almost by instinct. I guess it's habit.

WIFE: Never mind your habits. This is more important. Sugath and our girl don't seem to have hit it off too well. This afternoon he even yelled at her.

MUDALĀLI: Didn't I say from the very start, that might happen?

WIFE: That's not the point. Who knows if, in spite of being a monk, he's not in tow with some other girl?

MUDALĀLI: I don't think so.

WIFE: Think! One must have a brain to think! In the next day or two Sugath's mother will be here to get the money for paying the mortgage on her house. Tell her you'll give the money only if he'll marry the girl.

MUDALĀLI: But will my sister like the match?

WIFE: At first, you said he would never give up his monk's robes. Now you see he has. They are trapped. Can he rejoin the order? No. Say you'll give the money when the marriage is registered.

MUDALĀLI: But we initially said that we'll give the money if she gets the boy to give up his robes and come here.

WIFE: Yes, that's why, when we give the money, we also give our daughter. It shows an increase of our trust.

MUDALĀLI: It's good enough to say we will give this, we will give that. But what if we really have to give it?

WIFE: First, let's see if the girl gets well.

MUDALĀLI: Then what do we tell my sister?

WIFE: Tell her we plan to give our older daughter in marriage to Sugath. On the wedding day we will pay the mortgage on their house and property and give it to her unencumbered. After that, we will write the undertaking business over to Sugath. If he does not marry the girl, he gets nothing.

MUDALĀLI: (*opens the drawer*) What happened to the money that was in here? Sugath! Sugath! Where are you?

Sugath enters.

MUDALĀLI: Where's the money that was in this drawer?

SUGATH: Cousin Samson took it.

MUDALĀLI: You see, wife! Samson will be the ruin of this whole business!

WIFE: Let's wait and see how things work out.

Act three

The undertaker's shop. It is morning. The Mudalāli is seated at a table. Doregama Hāminē enters.

DOREGAMA HĀMINĒ: Ah! They tell me the boys have gone out to buy flowers. I wonder if they've gone far.

MUDALĀLI: No. It's close by here.

DOREGAMA HĀMINĒ: You see, brother, I waged a devil of a battle but finally got my boy to come to you. Now you pay off the mortgage on my house.

MUDALĀLI: I've been thinking too, sister. You know, it is very possible that Samson might try to create trouble for Sugath. Besides, one can't trust these young bachelors these days. The moment they are a little upset about something they chuck up their jobs. Now, if we make Sugath a part of our family that would take care of everything. He's of an age to be married. And, after all, he will not be marrying an unknown outsider.

DOREGAMA HĀMINĒ: I don't know what Sugath will have to say to all this.

MUDALĀLI: On questions like this, it is the parents who must consider their options and act. Otherwise, children go to ruin before you know it.

DOREGAMA HĀMINĒ: But the girl Sriya is not finished with her studies yet.

MUDALĀLI: I wasn't talking about my younger daughter.

DOREGAMA HĀMINĒ: Then?

MUDALĀLI: The older girl.

DOREGAMA HĀMINĒ: What do you mean? That girl is mad!

MUDALĀLI: She's not as mad as they say. She's been considerably better these past few days. The doctors say that once she marries she will be completely cured.

DOREGAMA HĀMINĒ: What! She'll be cured of her madness if she marries!

MUDALĀLI: Yes.

DOREGAMA HĀMINĒ: The doctors said that?

MUDALĀLI: You can check with any doctor you like, sister.

DOREGAMA HĀMINĒ: But brother that is impossible. The girl might not like it either. What if she drinks poison or does some mad thing?

MUDALĀLI: Well, I have made these suggestions in your interest, sister, because of our blood ties. Once married, the girl will be cured. The property will remain in the family. You may like to know that we've already had one or two other marriage proposals for the girl.

DOREGAMA HĀMINĒ: This is one thing I cannot do, even if it means I have to die a beggar in the street. Besides, the girl is lame in one leg.

MUDALĀLI: What does it matter if she limps a little. She'll always have a vehicle to travel in. She doesn't have to walk.

DOREGAMA HĀMINĒ: My son will never agree to it.

MUDALĀLI: If you allow the boy to do as he pleases, before you know it, there'll be some floosy hanging round his neck and finally they'll end up begging on the streets too. You know what happened in your own case. Do you remember how many Mudalālis were eager to marry you? But you were headstrong and chose to go with that musician. See what finally happened to you.

DOREGAMA HĀMINĒ: However that may be, this is not something I can do, brother.

MUDALĀLI: If you agree, the day the marriage is registered I will give you the money to pay off the mortgage on your house. After that, I will write this business in Sugath's name.

DOREGAMA HĀMINĒ: You never talked about a marriage when we first discussed the matter. You said that if I were to persuade the boy to give up his robes and come to work for you, you would give me the money.

MUDALĀLI: If he doesn't marry there's no guarantee that he will stay on here permanently.

DOREGAMA HĀMINĒ: I just can't bring myself to broach this to the boy. Why don't you tell him?

MUDALĀLI: I can't. Besides, the boy will never give me a straight answer.

DOREGAMA HĀMINĒ: If I bring this up now he might leave the shop completely and go somewhere far away.

MUDALĀLI: Just put it to him and see what he says. Besides, you know that if I give a lakh or two as dowry I'll have no problem giving the daughter in marriage to someone else.

DOREGAMA HĀMINĒ: If you had talked about the marriage at the very beginning I would not have persuaded the boy to give up his robes and come here.

MUDALĀLI: I don't know about all that. I've merely told you what might be done. Now don't blame me, later, saying I didn't give you money and that this property went out of the family, to outsiders. Ah, there comes your son. Just ask him how he feels about it. I shouldn't be here when he comes.

Sugath's voice can be heard outside. The Mudalāli exits.

SUGATH: Mother, have you been waiting long?

DOREGAMA HĀMINĒ: No son. I just got here. You seem very busy …

SUGATH: It's not too bad.

DOREGAMA HĀMINĒ: Son, I have a very important matter to discuss with you.

SUGATH: What is it?

DOREGAMA HĀMINĒ: You know my brother's elder daughter, Lakshmi?

SUGATH: Yes.

DOREGAMA HĀMINĒ: What do you feel about her?

SUGATH: When I see her, I feel like running back to the monastery.

DOREGAMA HĀMINĒ: We've been caught in a deadly trap, my son.

SUGATH: Why? What is it?

DOREGAMA HĀMINĒ: My brother and his wife got you here with ulterior motives.

SUGATH: That is to say?

DOREGAMA HĀMINĒ: I understand that if Lakshmi is married her illness will be cured. These people got you here hoping to marry her to you.

SUGATH: What! This is a deadly trap!

DOREGAMA HĀMINĒ: Only when the marriage is registered will they give me the money to pay the mortgage off on our house. After that, he'll write this business over to you. If you don't agree you may have to leave here.

SUGATH: I never dreamed such things could happen. Let's leave here right now, Mother. I'll do any kind of hard labor and we'll survive. We don't want this business—that girl, they say, is going to die in two months.

DOREGAMA HĀMINĒ: What? Are you saying that she'll live just two more months?

SUGATH: Yes.

DOREGAMA HĀMINĒ: How do you know that?

SUGATH: The doctors have said so. Newton and others know all about it. But they won't mention it to uncle and aunt—it would be too hard for them to take.

DOREGAMA HĀMINĒ: Just two months … Why, then there's no problem son …

SUGATH: Now what do you mean?

DOREGAMA HĀMINĒ: All you have to say is that you will marry her.

SUGATH: What? Are you asking me to marry a woman who is about to breathe her last?

DOREGAMA HĀMINĒ: That's not the point, son. Since they trapped us into this, what we must do is tie them up in knots and trap them in return.

SUGATH: No matter how many knots you tie, how can I marry a woman who is about to die?

DOREGAMA HĀMINĒ: Just listen to me for a moment. If we refuse them now, the whole point of giving up your robes and coming here would be lost. We'd lose our house too, for sure. Then what about all this property?

SUGATH: Mother, I'm sure that in two or three months I can get a job to teach music. After that, we can try to save the house.

DOREGAMA HĀMINĒ: Don't imagine it's that easy to get teaching posts. Besides, when have teachers ever had even a rupee or two to spare in an entire lifetime?

SUGATH: Then, what do you suggest I do, Mother?

DOREGAMA HĀMINĒ: Since they tricked us let us trick them in return.

SUGATH: How?

DOREGAMA HĀMINĒ: Sh … quiet now. We'll say you have agreed to marry her. But we'll also say that since there's still about two months before we perform the memorial ceremony for your dead father, that we can't have the wedding till all that is over. However, pretend you are going to marry her and act that way with the girl.

SUGATH: After that, what?

DOREGAMA HĀMINĒ: After that, when the disease gets really serious we'll register the marriage and get the money.

SUGATH: Then what?

DOREGAMA HĀMINĒ: Then after another week or two … Doctors aren't usually wrong son. After seven or eight days you'll be a bachelor again. And the money will be in our hands.

SUGATH: What if in the middle of all this business Lakshmi suddenly recovers?

DOREGAMA HĀMINĒ: This is not a curable illness, son.

SUGATH: But what if by some chance she does recover?

DOREGAMA HĀMINĒ: Recover? … If she recovers—I'll take care of that.

SUGATH: By going to play a trick on them if we actually get caught in this trap, it will mean a lifetime of suffering for me.

DOREGAMA HĀMINĒ: Son, you know I love you. It's that now I am like a beggar out on the street. If the girl dies shortly after the wedding, then there's no problem. The marriage is over, and that's all that matters.

SUGATH: But I'll be a widower then.

DOREGAMA HĀMINĒ: So what? You don't have to hang a board round your neck saying you're a widower? We'll tell them to make the marriage a secret one.

SUGATH: I can't do it, Mother. I must leave this instant.

DOREGAMA HĀMINĒ: Son, you and I are like two fish caught in a net. Oh god! In this unending *samsaric* cycle of being, may I never again have to suffer like this for want of money! Just think a moment, son. As soon as you leave these premises any possibility of help from this family is gone. What then?

SUGATH: I can't do it, Mother. I'll leave and never set foot on this soil again. (*He runs out but stops at the back of the stage as he hears the song of the narrator.*)

NARRATOR:

With soft words and the milk of her breasts she fed you
And now walks weeping scalding tears of grief.
How will she live if she never again sets eyes on you?
May you attain the peace of nibbana mother dear!

SUGATH: (*walking slowly back*) All right. What do you want me to do?

DOREGAMA HĀMINĒ: All you have to do is agree to the marriage and act as if you are engaged. Once we get the money … How can we alone be moral when everyone around us subscribes to an amoral life?

SUGATH: Let's say everything happens as you predict. Then, after that, will you agree to my wishes?

DOREGAMA HĀMINĒ: After that, I will never oppose you on anything, son.

SUGATH: Then say you will not object to Sarasvathi?

DOREGAMA HĀMINĒ: Sa … ras … va … thi …!

SUGATH: That's what I said! You only see things from your point of view.

DOREGAMA HĀMINĒ: Well, what can I do? All right, I won't object to her. Now, shall I tell my brother you agree to the marriage?

SUGATH: Tell him whatever you wish. But don't ever again object to Sa … ra …

Lakshmi enters. She scatters money around her.

DOREGAMA HĀMINĒ: (*to Sugath*) Now say a few loving words to her.

SUGATH: Loving?

DOREGAMA HĀMINĒ: Pretend.

MUDALĀLI: Ah, sister! Why do you stand out there in the shop? Do come into the house. Lakshmi … Lakshmi … Come inside.

DOREGAMA HĀMINĒ: Let her stay a while, brother. The young people should have a chance to talk and get to know each other.

MUDALĀLI: Ah … Is that's so … Very good. Very good … Then you come and have a cup of tea with us, sister.

Sugath and Lakshmi look at each other in silence.

SUGATH: Lakshmi?

LAKSHMI: Yes?

SUGATH: How far is it from here to the hospital?

LAKSHMI: Well, let's see. The sound of men dying at the hospital can be heard here and the sound of coffins being made here can be heard at the hospital. The men who come to hospital buy their coffins from here—and the men who buy the coffins go to the hospital over there. From the hospital—to here. From here—to the hospital … Do you know I burnt all my brides?

SUGATH: What? Ah yes. So, you burned them.

LAKSHMI: Mother told me that she was going to buy me clothes just like what those brides were wearing.

SUGATH: Whatever for? … Ah, yes, yes … she must have told you.

LAKSHMI: What for? Why, the other day a bride had died, and they brought her here dressed in her bridal clothes.

SUGATH: What about it?

LAKSHMI: They put her in a beautiful coffin and took her away. When mother talked about bridal clothes I thought of her. Mother also said I should stay here and talk to you, Cousin Sugath. But I feel shy …

SUGATH: Why?

LAKSHMI: I don't know. I feel shy. Cousin Sugath, do you want me to stay here or do you not?

SUGATH: On no, do stay.

LAKSHMI: Do you see that hawk, up there … He's also looking for a bride. Oh no. He's looking for a coffin. No. He's looking for a coffin in which to carry his bride. No, he's looking for a bride to bring him a coffin.

SUGATH: He's looking for a bride amidst the coffins!

LAKSHMI: He's looking for a coffin amidst the brides.

Sarasvathi enters.

SARASVATHI: I was on my way to class. Why is that crazy creature always here? If you hang around with her too much you might go crazy too!

SUGATH: Lakshmi go home. I have work to do.

LAKSHMI: Then why did you say you wanted me to stay? Ask that woman also to go away.

SUGATH: She has come to buy some flowers.

LAKSHMI: But I can't bear the sight of her.

SARASVATHI: Can't bear to see me! I wonder why?

LAKSHMI: This is my cousin, Sugath. (*She strokes his face.*)

SARASVATHI: Oh, is that how it is? Shall I leave, Sugath?

SUGATH: I told you to leave here, Lakshmi.

LAKSHMI: (*to Sarasvathi*) Get out! Take your flowers and get out of here. This is our shop.

SARASVATHI: What a foul-mouthed witch! You get out yourself! You lame loony.

LAKSHMI: What … (*She runs out.*)

SARASVATHI: It looks as if she's suffering from marriage madness!

SUGATH: I feel sorry for her, Sarasvathi. They say she won't live long.

SARASVATHI: How's that?

SUGATH: They say her madness will intensify in two more months.

SARASVATHI: Good god! How do you know that it's not infectious?

SUGATH: No no, it's not an infectious illness. It's something wrong with her head.

SARASVATHI: Dear Sugath, I keep telling you; please don't stay here any longer.

SUGATH: I will stay here exactly two months. That's all Sarasvathi.

SARASVATHI: And after that, what?

SUGATH: After that I'll go somewhere else.

SARASVATHI: I came to give you some good news.

SUGATH: What is it?

SARASVATHI: It looks as if something is likely to work out in a month or two so we can go to India to study music. If you can come too it would be wonderful!

SUGATH: In two months I may be able to come.

SARASVATHI: Is that really true?

SUGATH: If everything works out as I expect it to, I will definitely come.

SARASVATHI: How wonderful! We can both study music there and when we return we can always find something to do.

SUGATH: I've told Mother about you, Sarasvathi.

SARASVATHI: Good god! She must have been furious and scolded you roundly.

SUGATH: No, she didn't say anything.

SARASVATHI: That's very surprising! When we meet in the village she glares at me. I never dreamed that your mother would ever approve of someone like me.

SUGATH: All this will be over in two months.

NEWTON: (*enters*) Mr. Sugath.

SARASVATHI: I'm off, Sugath.

NEWTON: Who was that, sir?

SUGATH: Er … she… she came to get some flowers.

NEWTON: That's for sure! Didn't I see the armfuls of flowers she carried away! You, appear such a saint but what a devil you are! Ha … ha … ha … But let's get going. They've already brought a fresh corpse. He's a famous artist. There's nothing left of him to embalm, however. Hardly an ounce of flesh on the poor guy!

Mudalāli enters hurriedly, followed by his wife.

WIFE: Where are you running off to now, without finishing our talk about that matter?

MUDALĀLI: Can't you see? They've brought in a corpse.

DOREGAMA HĀMINĒ: Then I must be going too.

Samson enters with a bag and helmet and is about to leave through the side door.

WIFE: Samson, where are you going?

SAMSON: I have nowhere to go. It's the high road for me.

MUDALĀLI: The high road! What's the matter with you?

SAMSON: Nothing is wrong with me. The matter is with you and Mother.

MUDALĀLI: With us! Say any damn thing you have to say Samson. Stop talking in riddles.

SAMSON: It's my being at home that is a burden on everyone … You couldn't write this shop over to me Father, not even just in name. But now you are all prepared to give it to a rank outsider.

WIFE: An outsider? Who said so?

SAMSON: Who? Father said so. I'm asking you, Father, didn't you tell Aunt Doregama that in a day or two you are going to write this shop over to Sugath? Didn't you say that? Your words now stick in your throat …

MUDALĀLI: You don't understand anything Samson. Stop braying like a donkey.

SAMSON: Yes, I've become the donkey. That renegade monk has now become a horse!

WIFE: Sa … m … son …!

SAMSON: I will never again set foot in this place. However, keep in mind that there will now be someone who has declared war on this undertaking business. I will be waiting out there.

WIFE: Samson …!

Black-out. Blue cyclorama.[29] *The narrator passes from right to left singing the following verse.*

You who love your children, mother goddesses
The night is full of dreams, the dark, endless.
In dreams the body burns, no salve left to rub.
All gods turn into demons in this kali Yug.

Act four

The undertaker's shop, two months later. The Mudalāli and his wife are seated and talking.

WIFE: Our son, Samson, has come back.

MUDALĀLI: What! Samson is here? What trouble has he got into now?

WIFE: Oh no. Nothing like that.

MUDALĀLI: The two months I've spent without seeing him seem like two years of respite.

WIFE: The boy has changed considerably. I told him the whole story. Lakshmi is now well, and he was so happy to see that. He may be pig-headed, but he does care very much for the family. (*She looks around.*) Where is Sugath?

MUDALĀLI: He left with a corpse.

WIFE: (*laughing*) The mother and son both imagine that we truly intend to give our girl to them!

MUDALĀLI: I don't know what to do. How can we now tell my sister that we are not going to give the girl to Sugath?

WIFE: What! Are you suggesting that now, when she is completely well, we give our girl in marriage to that beggar, and with a dowry to boot!

MUDALĀLI: But the girl was completely cured only after she began to associate with Sugath. Besides, they are family, our own blood. We are kin.

WIFE: Don't bring up that talk of blood and kin and this and that. Can we allow our girl to become a destitute? And that when there is a lawyer eager to marry her?

MUDALĀLI: What did Mr. Victor say?

WIFE: He is very keen to marry our daughter. He was here yesterday, too, flirting with her.

MUDALĀLI: I thought that lawyer was keen on our younger daughter.

WIFE: That may have been so because the man is keen to marry into our family. When one is a lawyer, that's the way lawyers are. One looks for a family that has money and property. You don't choose a woman off the streets. When I saw that Lakshmi was cured of her illness, I put the idea to him in a roundabout fashion. He seems willing. We might have to give a fairly big dowry, however.

MUDALĀLI: But our daughter is expecting to marry Sugath, isn't she?

WIFE: Yes, that's what she's hoping for. It's true we bought her bridal clothes saying she was marrying Sugath.

MUDALĀLI: If we tell her about this lawyer now, what if she gets upset and sick again?

WIFE: Don't tell the child anything until we get ourselves free of Sugath. Let's behave as if we are going ahead with plans for the wedding, just as we promised.

MUDALĀLI: I've been sitting here thinking what I should say to my sister when she comes now. What shall I do?

WIFE: You don't have to do anything. Leave Samson the task of getting rid of Sugath. You and I should act as if we knew nothing of all this.

MUDALĀLI: Leave it to Samson?

WIFE: Yes.

MUDALĀLI: What? You let that madman handle such a delicate task! Before you know it, we might end up with a corpse on our hands. Don't you ever use your head?

WIFE: I have suffered so much over this illness and now at last got our daughter cured. Let me handle the rest of this business. You just sit and wait.

MUDALĀLI: What if my sister asks for the money that we promised her earlier? What can I say to her?

WIFE: We said we'd give the money only after the wedding.

Sugath enters.

MUDALĀLI: Ah, you've returned very quickly. Newton drives our new hearse far too fast. Well then, you can look after things here. I must go supervise the making of the coffins. If one doesn't stand over them, these carpenters waste so much wood.

He leaves with his wife and Doregama Hāminē comes in from the other side.

DOREGAMA HĀMINĒ: Son!

SUGATH: Yes.

DOREGAMA HĀMINĒ: Where is my brother?

SUGATH: There they are, making great preparations for the wedding.

DOREGAMA HĀMINĒ: Who would have thought that the girl would get well so easily. I thought she'd get worse by the day. Now it looks as if the doctors were quite wrong.

SUGATH: That's why I refused at the very beginning. Now I'm the one who finally gets caught in this deadly noose.

DOREGAMA HĀMINĒ: Well, when you come to think of it, now that her madness is cured, there's nothing wrong in your actually marrying her.

SUGATH: Yes, I know. Everyone wanted me to be the sacrificial lamb! Now don't say I didn't warn you. If I have to actually marry her, then the day after the wedding I leave and don't imagine you will ever set eyes on me again.

DOREGAMA HĀMINĒ: Son, we have just one week before all our lands become forfeit. If we don't finalize things now, our house and lands will all be gone, and I will be out on the streets.

SUGATH: But now there will be no more deceptions. If I marry her I'm trapped for life. I will have to spend the rest of my life among these coffins with this woman who they said was going to die any day!

DOREGAMA HĀMINĒ: Son, now she is completely cured.

SUGATH: Who can tell if the illness won't come back? How can one dare to even step out on the street with such a woman?

DOREGAMA HĀMINĒ: Her horoscope, however, is a very powerful one.

SUGATH: That's a lie! They've given you someone else's horoscope. According to Lakshmi's horoscope they say the man she marries will die too.

DOREGAMA HĀMINĒ: Good heavens! Who told you that?

SUGATH: Oh, Newton and others know all the details.

DOREGAMA HĀMINĒ: In that case we certainly don't want this marriage! I'll tell my brother that we can't go ahead with it.

SUGATH: What then?

DOREGAMA HĀMINĒ: Well then, I'll have to take what comes, even if it means a life of beggary. O ye gods! What karmic fate is working itself out that all this is now collapsing on our heads!

SUGATH: If our bad karma is about to work itself out, then there is no escape.

DOREGAMA HĀMINĒ: We are both of us, straws caught in a great flood.

SUGATH: These people have made all preparations for the wedding.

DOREGAMA HĀMINĒ: Well, let's see. This horrible fate will befall only if she survives after the wedding.

SUGATH: Mother, what are you saying? How can you play with people's lives like this, just for money?

DOREGAMA HĀMINĒ: When men have played games with my life, for money, how can I think in terms of goodness and charity? I am not the daughter of a demon, son, but I, too, am human.

SUGATH: What shall we do now?

DOREGAMA HĀMINĒ: The only thing to do now is to go ahead with the wedding as promised. I will look after the rest.

SUGATH: First, they said, they would register the marriage in secret. Now they are making plans for a big wedding celebration.

DOREGAMA HĀMINĒ: I'll tell my brother that since your father has been dead so recently, that they should have the wedding with the least amount of fuss and no publicity. Let me go in and see them.

She leaves and Sarasvathi enters.

SUGATH: Ah Sarasvathi! I've been waiting for days now, wondering why you hadn't dropped in.

SARASVATHI: What's the use of my coming here anymore? I've come now, only because it will be the last time.

SUGATH: The last time? Why do you say that?

SARASVATHI: It is because we have been so close since the time we were children, that I couldn't bring myself to break the bond between us. That's why I kept hoping. Otherwise, I didn't have to run behind you Sugath.

SUGATH: So, what has changed now?

SARASVATHI: Changed? Had I known that you had come here because you were so greedy for your uncle's money, and that you had agreed to marry that madwoman just for that, I would not have set foot in here.

SUGATH: Who says I'm marrying that madwoman?

SARASVATHI: Who says so? Hm … Are you still trying to lie to me? I never dreamed that you were such a low-down scheming rotter, Sugath.

SUGATH: I have not lied to you, Sarasvathi.

SARASVATHI: Not lied! The wedding is to take place in a day or two and you still say you have not lied!

SUGATH: You don't understand anything, Sarasvathi. That's all a deception, a lie.

SARASVATHI: A lie! People don't deceive when they marry. It is to me that you have lied. I never dreamed you would change in this way, and all for money.

SUGATH: I have not changed, Sarasvathi. How can I explain all this to you?

SARASVATHI: There is nothing to explain. You've decided to do this because you believe it's in your best interests. I came to bid you goodbye. I'm about to leave for …

SUGATH: About to leave for … ? What do you mean?

SARASVATHI: Yes, we are going to India the day after tomorrow.

SUGATH: The day after tomorrow!

SARASVATHI: Yes, Krishnan is coming too. You remember Krishnan?

SUGATH: Krishnan?

SARASVATHI: Yes.

SUGATH: In another week all this will be over. Don't go to India till then, please Sarasvathi.

SARASVATHI: Are you asking me to wait to attend your wedding? My folks at home are pressuring me to get married before I leave for India. I have decided to marry Krishnan.

SUGATH: Sarasvathi, there is nothing at all between Lakshmi and me.

Lakshmi enters dressed in bridal attire.

SARASVATHI: Nothing between you and Lakshmi! Well, there she comes, all dressed up and ready for the wedding ceremony! I'm leaving. (*She leaves.*)

SUGATH: Sarasvathi! (*sees Lakshmi and scolds her*) Why the hell did you have to come in here?

Lakshmi retreats slowly backwards.

LAKSHMI: Ever since I was a child everyone has appeared to me as a demon. All around me were coffins. Amidst those coffins the only person who seemed human was your mother. It was only your mother who showed any compassion for me. I don't remember what happened to me in the recent past. But now I know that I'm once again, just a lonely cripple, lost among these coffins and corpses.

Narrator chants from the back.

We were two squirrels in the jungle when
Our young one into the swirling waters fell.
How hard you tried and tried to save him then
Oh husband dear, do you desert him now?[30]

Sugath deeply moved, comes up to Lakshmi and takes her by the hand.

SUGATH: Lakshmi, let's go home.

DOREGAMA HĀMINĒ: (*entering*) What does she say now, this witch, who has come to destroy us all?

SUGATH: Don't say that, Mother. We are all creatures of flesh and blood. Lakshmi is human too.

DOREGAMA HĀMINĒ: What! What are you saying now?

SUGATH: I have decided. I'm going to marry Lakshmi.

DOREGAMA HĀMINĒ: And what about the horoscope predictions?

SUGATH: If something is fated to happen there is no way to stop it, Mother.

DOREGAMA HĀMINĒ: I know. You have decided to do this as an act of revenge against me, isn't that so son?

SUGATH: No, I truly feel compassion for Lakshmi.

DOREGAMA HĀMINĒ: Well, if everything is going to be solved so easily, good! That's a relief anyway.

SAMSON: *(enters)* Ha cousin! So! You indulge in every depravity, run around town with loose women, and now come here to find a bride, do you? Get out of here—right now.

SUGATH: What?

DOREGAMA HĀMINĒ: What is this? What are you saying Samson, my child?

SAMSON: *(ignoring her and addressing Sugath)* You think you are going to marry my sister, do you? Ha! Do you imagine man that we will give our sister to a rotter like you? You can leave this house right now!

DOREGAMA HĀMINĒ: What are you saying? Well, it was not with your permission that we came here in the first place.

The Mudalalai, his wife and Newton come running in.

WIFE: What's going on?

DOREGAMA HĀMINĒ: You see what's going on! It's not enough what we do for this family. Now we have to hear abuse too!

SAMSON: Abuse is it? Papa, you intend to make this rotter your son-in-law don't you? Do you know what he's up to?

DOREGAMA HĀMINĒ: Why, what has he done?

SAMSON: What has he done? He has been dancing a jig with that woman called Sarasvathi who gallivants all over town. The whole town knows about it. She has even stayed here in this shop on several occasions. You'll know how far the affair has gone when she turns up here on the wedding day! Are you so shameless as to even think of giving my sister to him?

WIFE: Good heavens! Who ever knew of such a thing!

SAMSON: That's why they say that a monk who has shed his robes is like a potsherd. It won't stick back on the pot and the earth will not bond with it.

DOREGAMA HĀMINĒ: This is a total falsehood; something concocted by Samson.

SAMSON: A falsehood! Ask Newton. Didn't that creature Sarasvathi come here to the coffin shop to meet this man?

Newton is silent.

Tell the truth, man.

Newton is silent.

MUDALĀLI: Speak, Newton, Is this true?

NEWTON: Yes, that young woman carrying a violin would come in here almost every day.

WIFE: Yes, yes. I too now remember her coming in here. Good heavens! What a disgrace! Is it to such a man that we were intending to give our daughter? Some kind of a nephew he is!

DOREGAMA HĀMINĒ: O gods! This is a crime! You people didn't allow this boy to be where he was. Now you are trying to destroy him!

MUDALĀLI: How can we give our daughter to a man with such a reputation? What if the woman barges in on the wedding day and accuses him in public like Chinchimānavikā accused the Buddha?[31]

WIFE: No, no. Even if you cut me up and throw me into a river or the ocean, I will not give my daughter—not to such a man!

DOREGAMA HĀMINĒ: Why do you perpetrate such slander? Go question that woman and find out the truth of the matter.

SUGATH: Sarasvathi is getting married tomorrow and going to India.

SAMSON: You see! How would he know all those details if he didn't know her well. You said just now that it was all a lie.

WIFE: No, no, definitely not. We will not give you our daughter. How can we give this sick girl to a man of loose character?

SAMSON: If you keep this kind of character to run this shop, people will stop coming even to buy coffins.

LAKSHMI: If Cousin Sugath leaves, then I too am going with him.

DOREGAMA HĀMINĒ: Where do you think you are going?

LAKSHMI: Wherever Cousin Sugath goes I will go with him.

SUGATH: Yes, Lakshmi, let us leave here. (*They are about to leave.*)

SAMSON: Oh … no … no … just a moment …

DOREGAMA HĀMINĒ: What? You plan to marry her? Are you going to hang this lame, mad-woman round your neck and for nothing?

WIFE: (*pulling Lakshmi to her*) You think we'll give her to you? No such luck! We don't need that disrobed monk. There are plenty of other gentlemen eager to marry her. (*to Lakshmi*) Go on, go into the house.

LAKSHMI: No, I will not go. I will only go with Cousin Sugath.

SAMSON: What did you say? Go in this instant or you know what will happen. (*He drags Lakshmi by the hand to take her in.*) And if this fellow happens to be still here in this shop when I come back, you had better have a coffin ready for him too. (*He leaves, dragging Lakshmi away.*)

WIFE: Heavens! What a near escape from a deadly trap! (*She goes inside.*)

DOREGAMA HĀMINĒ: You will all pay for this crime, someday. Let's see how you are going to find other sons-in-law!

MUDALĀLI: If your son had been of good character none of this would have happened. (*He leaves with Newton.*)

DOREGAMA HĀMINĒ: (*to Sugath*) I warned you, didn't I? I told you that wicked creature Sarasvathi would get you into trouble someday. Now it's all over. All our efforts wasted. We are washed away like sticks in a flood. Sha! Well, let's go, let's go home.

SUGATH: No, I'm not going anywhere.

DOREGAMA HĀMINĒ: What! Are you going to wait here and be murdered by that bum?

SUGATH: I will not move from here even if I have to die.

DOREGAMA HĀMINĒ: Now, we are caught in their trap. Well, I will wreak vengeance on them, someday. (*pulls him by the hand*) Come on, let's get out of here.

SUGATH: I told you, I am not leaving.

DOREGAMA HĀMINĒ: O god! (*moves to the spotlight on left*) I've lost everything. Now, I lose you too.

Sugath moves to the rear of the stage out of his mother's view. Death-Demon-Saima enters and stands in the spotlight at the right of stage.

DOREGAMA HĀMINĒ: (*talking softly almost to herself*) For years after I married, I did not have a child. It was only after I had walked to all the shrines in the country making vows that I conceived you, my son. When you were a child I looked after you like my two eyes. I remember once, around midnight you had convulsions. Your father was not home. It was raining hard enough to strip the berries off the trees. In that pelting rain I took you in my arms and ran all the way to the hospital at Doregama. My son … (*realizes that Sugath is not to be seen*)

Death-Demon-Saima walks across the stage.

My son? Where is my son? Where is my son?

Death-Demon-Saima remains silent. Doregama Hāminē walks back stage and runs back instantly, screaming. Lakshmi, mad once more now, comes dancing in a trance, on stage. Doregama Hāminē collapses beside a coffin weeping …

Son!

NARRATOR:

Will the spells of devilish demons now be broken?
Will the sorcerer's magic fetters now be cut?
Will the demon spells that bound you now be loosened?
Or will the laws of insane devils rule the world?

The end

****

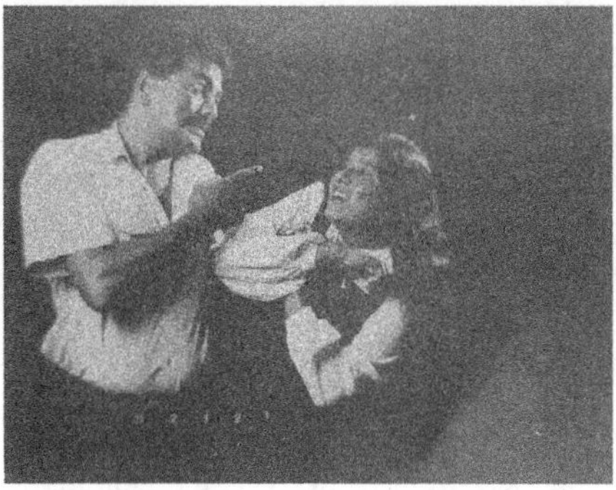

PHOTOGRAPHS 1.1 Lakshmi and Samson in *Goddess of Illusion*. Photograph by Sisira Wijethunga

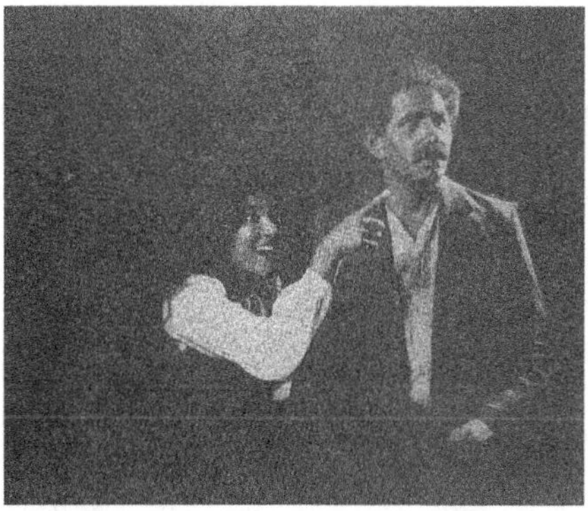

PHOTOGRAPHS 1.2 Lakshmi and Mudalāli in *Goddess of Illusion*. Photograph by Sisira Wijethunga

Notes

1 Hindu gods are familiar to Sinhala Buddhists, since over the years they have been assimilated as a pantheon of lesser deities who have the power to intervene in the daily life of humans. This is a role that, according to Doctrinal Buddhism, the Buddha, being human, does not perform.
2 A Sinhala word for businessman.
3 Benevolent deities that shower blessings on humans. Sirikatha is the goddess of prosperity and one of the consorts of Vishnu, while Sarasvathi, the goddess of learning, is the other consort of Vishnu.
4 Kali in her merciful form as Badra Kali and Durga the fierce goddess, the two wives of god Shiva are invoked here.
5 Gods associated with death and destruction.
6 The actors are lined up as the deities.

7 Kruta, Dvapara and Kali, are the names of three periods (yugas) or eons. The Kali-yug, or the era of the goddess Kali in her destructive form, is a period of chaos and degeneration and marks the final destruction of the world as we know.
8 Sammata was the title given to the first ruler of the world to be chosen by the people. So, Maha Sammata can be translated as the first great ruler to be chosen by the people.
9 It is the Sinhala name for Vaisravana or a demon king who is often placated in ritual exorcist ceremonies.
10 Elephant tusks are often placed on either side of the coffin. They are symbols of high status and wealth and so are often hired by the family of the dead person for the occasion.
11 A term by which businessmen are addressed.
12 Hāminē signifies the lady of the house. Also, a form of address to one's wife.
13 Here the shift to calling her "woman" not Hāminē indicates his growing anger at his wife's talk.
14 A nickname that means Simon, god of the dead.
15 An ironic dig at fish shop owners in Sri Lanka who, it is said, use formalin to preserve their fish when they don't have refrigeration facilities.
16 In the text, Samson uses the western term for Father rather than the Sinhala word *thatha*, suggesting the degree of his alienation from his father's lower-middle-class world.
17 All lay Buddhists observe the Five Precepts, but on full moon days, some (especially older women), observe a more rigorous form, which is eight precepts.
18 Traditionally, houses were built by the individual from his own savings or inherited. They were mortgaged only in dire circumstances and thus a cause of considerable humiliation.
19 It is an idiomatic way of saying "one can try to hide a dirty dish by covering it with a lid but it is of no use."
20 This is from the Ummanga Jataka. Pinguttara is an unlucky youth who is given the beautiful, and very lucky daughter of his teacher as his wife. He abandons her on his way home leaving her stranded on a fig tree. She is found by the king and becomes his chief queen named Udumbara.
21 The "Triple Gem" or "Three Jewels" is an image used to sum up the tripartite nature of the religion that consists of the Buddha, the teacher; the Dhamma: Doctrine or Teachings; and the Sangha: or community of monks who will teach the doctrine to others. The phrase "May the Triple Gem be your refuge" is often used in popular parlance as a blessing—similar to saying "May God bless you."
22 Monks are usually laid out in coffins lined in saffron yellow, which is the color of a monk's robe.
23 Translation: "In a similar manner in which a flock of cranes with white wings would fly away in fear of the black clouds …" Verse from *Thera gatha*, Poems of Buddhist Bukkhus. This poem is attributed to Sappaka Thero.
24 In certain Sinhala-speaking contexts, people did not use the first person possessive terms to address and speak about one's parents. It was a sign of respect. Hence, when Sugath refers to "our" father here, he is referring to his father.
25 The popular term that lay people use to address young monks.
26 Lakshmi uses the Sinhala word, "*Korā*" here. It is now considered to be a highly offensive term. Yet, given the time period in which the play was written and given Lakshmi's socially and psychologically marginalized status, she uses this term.
27 A reference to the Pattini story where the goddess gives her anklet to her husband to sell. He is accused of having stolen it and put to death. Angered by the falsehood, deceit, and the killing of her husband by the King of Pandi, Pattini tears out her breast, and flings it at the city, which is then consumed in flames.

28 This is a stanza about the victory of the Buddha over the forces of Mara, demon of death. The verse is now also sung at weddings to provide blessings and protection to the bridal couple.
29 Blue light on a white wall in the back.
30 Lines from a popular folk song. The verse is part of Yasodhara's lament as she mourns her husband's departure when he renounced family and kingdom in his quest to become a Buddha.
31 The story of the prostitute Chincamānavikā who was instigated by a group of ascetic opponents to his teachings to make a public accusation that she was the mistress of the Buddha.

***

K.B. Herath, a veteran theater director and playwright, began his theatrical career in the late 1960s. His plays, which often combine traditional performance methods with more realistic theatrical techniques, bring onto stage retellings of historical narratives and portrayals of contemporary life. He has written and directed many plays in Sinhala and won numerous awards for the best playwright and director. He was given "Naatya Keerthi," the Lifetime Achievement Award, at the State Drama Festival in 2019. His plays offer a critique of power and the corruption of rulers and grapples with a topic that is curiously absent from much of Sinhala theatre, the war. He explores the place of women in a patriarchal system, bravely probing issues related to gender and sexuality in several of his plays. Some of his works include *Naga Gurula* (1992), *Dona Kathirina* (1995), *Deveni Mahinda/ Mahinda the Second* (1998), *Vasudeva* (1999) and *Jagan Ma* (2009). K.B. Herath's work invites us to rethink history and thereby offers an alternative view of it.

THE BEARER OF WOES (DUKGANNĀRĀLA 1989)

Prasannajith Abeysuriya

Characters

MAN
WOMAN
DIRECTOR
SPONSOR
1ST ACTOR
2ND ACTOR
3RD ACTOR
1ST ACTRESS
2ND ACTRESS
3RD ACTRESS
USHER

Act 1

A bell rings and the curtain slowly opens. Only the cyclorama is lit. Shadows of actors can be seen silhouetted against it. They dance to the strains of soft music. A voice sings off stage.

It's the cool season, the season of rains
I will relax in this rainy season
It is spring in life's garden
Sweet scents flood the air
Let's float away on a cloud
a cloud …

While the dancers move to the music on stage, a disturbance occurs at the side entrance to the auditorium. Someone is at the door demanding to be let in. The usher opens the door.

A woman carrying a child rushes in. While the dance continues on stage this scene takes place by the entrance door (up left). The area is lit only with the usher's flashlight.

USHER: OK. OK. Come in if you must. But please go in quietly and sit down if you wish to see the performance.

WOMAN: I don't want to see any performance. I just want to stay here for a little while.

USHER: This is a theater. There's a show going on.

WOMAN: I don't care what's going on. I just want to stay here for a little while.

SPONSOR: (*Who has financed the show, walks up to the door from inside the auditorium.*) No. That's impossible. Kindly leave and don't cause any trouble.

The usher tries to push her out and close the door.

WOMAN: Please, please don't close the door on me. If I step outside I'm finished.

SPONSOR: What kind of a trouble-maker are you? If you wish to see the show, come in and sit down. If not, kindly leave.

WOMAN: Please let me stay here a while. I beg you let me stay. If I go back outside I'm done for!

The usher again tries to throw her out and close the door. She steps further in and continues to plead with him. Meanwhile, the actors on stage become aware of the disturbance. They stop their dance to look at what's going on. The Director of the show now comes on stage.

DIRECTOR: Lights! Let's have some lights in the auditorium!

The lights go on in the auditorium and the woman is clearly seen half way inside.

DIRECTOR: What's the problem? Doesn't she have a ticket?

SPONSOR: She doesn't want to see the show. But she won't go away either—insists on staying inside.

DIRECTOR: (*to the woman*) What's the matter? What is it? Are you alone? What! You have a child with you too?

Meanwhile, the woman glances nervously at the door.

What's the matter lady, have you left someone or something behind?

WOMAN: No.

DIRECTOR: Then what is it? A robber?

WOMAN: It's my child's father.

DIRECTOR: Who? Where is he?

WOMAN: He's probably at the door waiting for me.

DIRECTOR: Why? Is anything wrong? Why did you run in here alone?

WOMAN: He was beating me. I grabbed my child and ran. He chased me all the way here. I came inside as it was my only means of escape.

1ST ACTOR: *(from on stage)* The bully! Hey! Is the guy outside? We'll beat him up and make him run!

DIRECTOR: Please! Calm down! Let's go into this matter in a reasonable rational way. Now tell us, where are you from?

WOMAN: From the shanty housing by the canal.

SPONSOR: This audience has come to see a play. The actors are about to perform. Please leave and let them get on with their show. Sort out your personal problems in your own home.

WOMAN: Don't ask me to go outside, please. If he catches me I'm dead.

DIRECTOR: If you carry on like this, young lady, it's I who will be dead! If this performance doesn't take place the audience will kill me. Not to mention the actors on one side and the sponsor on the other—all out for my blood. What do you expect me to do? Please leave.

WOMAN: Have you no heart? If something happens to me what will become of this child? (*She weeps.*)

DIRECTOR: Don't give me one more headache, lady! Please go. Don't force me to have you thrown out. What is the world coming to if a man can't come to the theater and enjoy an evening's respectable entertainment?

1ST ACTRESS: Hurry up. Do whatever you have to do and let's get on with the performance. I have to go home alone after the show tonight.

1ST ACTOR: Don't worry. You won't die from a short walk home alone. You call that a problem? Look what this woman has to face!

SPONSOR: Such questions are irrelevant. Throw the woman out and let's get on with the show.

1ST ACTOR: Hold it! Just a minute! Our play can be shown again on any other night. But this is a question of life and death for this woman.

2ND ACTRESS: True. We can't just look away and do nothing.

3RD ACTRESS: Why not try to settle this matter before it gets out of hand?

DIRECTOR: (*To audience*) Please forgive us. Bear with us till we settle this matter. We'll start the performance all over again as soon as this little problem is solved. Will the Sponsor please come up to the stage for a moment?

The Director and Sponsor talk in whispers, step down from the stage and walk towards the woman. To the Woman:

Come along now. We'll walk out with you.

They walk to the door but on seeing the man standing outside the woman runs back into the auditorium.

SPONSOR: You have nothing to be afraid of. If anything happens we'll go to the Police.

The man now pushes his way in.

MAN: No one needs to go to the Police. This is a private family matter. (*To the woman*) Are you coming or not—right now?

SPONSOR: You see. We can't really interfere in this. Please leave. After all he is your man.

WOMAN: I beg you have pity. I can't go with him.

SPONSOR: (*to the Man*) Look here, fellow. Take her and get out, will you? We must go on with the show.

MAN: Who's stopping you? If you have such an important performance going on, throw that woman out.

SPONSOR: When your wife creeps in here saying you are trying to kill her, can we throw her out?

MAN: How come you feel so warmly towards her? What's eating you?

SPONSOR: I have no special interest. All we want is to get on with our performance. I've spent a lot of money organizing this show. That's what's eating me.

MAN: You don't have to take on other people's headaches. (*to the woman*) Come on, let's go home.

WOMAN: I won't. I can't. I won't die for nothing.

MAN: I don't want to be a murderer either. Come along now.

WOMAN: Leave me to live my life, and you go worship at any shrine you want.

MAN: Whatever shrine I may go to—I can't leave you now. Even if I left you I can't abandon my child.

WOMAN: You should have thought about all that before you decided to have a child.

MAN: I can't stay here all day talking. Come on now. Let's go home.

WOMAN: No. I won't go.

MAN: I'm telling you kindly, come on, let's go. (*He pulls her by the hand.*)

WOMAN: I can't! I won't! Look what he's doing to me!

While they struggle members of the cast jump down off the stage and break up the fight.

1ST ACTOR: Aren't you ashamed man, to show off your muscle power on a woman?

MAN: Since you know nothing of the truth of the matter, I suppose its natural you should see it that way.

DIRECTOR: It looks as if there is a more serious problem here. But I don't know what to do. If all this had happened outside, we could have closed the doors and got on with the show. But now the problem is inside and with us. Can we calmly get back on stage and continue our performance while such searing conflicts are taking place before our very eyes? I, for one, cannot. Therefore, without finding a solution to this problem I can't continue with the play.

SPONSOR: Do whatever you want. Solve the problem anyway you know and let's get on with the show. Only, don't take too long or I'll have to get into the act myself!

DIRECTOR: Right! Give us just a little time, sir.

The Sponsor gets down off the stage and walks away. The usher follows behind. The Director goes up to the Man.

Now please tell us what is the problem here?

MAN: If you fellows only knew the kind of problems we have, you would write not one but ten plays!

DIRECTOR: Yes, yes, we understand. (*to the Woman*) Now you calm down too. Cool your anger, forget your fears and together tell us your story. We might be able to help you resolve this conflict.

1ST ACTOR: We'll join in too if necessary. We are very good at impromptu miming performances.

MAN: Well, perhaps it's just as well you should know the facts. I won't be made a villain for no fault of mine. I'll tell you our story so you people can understand my position in all this.

The Director leads the man on stage. The actors sit down on either side. The man begins his story. From this point the story becomes the play. The actors help with songs and mimes.

MAN: I first met her near the hospital.

As he talks only his face is lit. The cyclorama now lights up and against it the actors enact a hospital scene.

I went to see a friend that day. On leaving his room I was aware of a disturbance near the gate. People were crowding round someone.

The left side of the stage lights up. A crowd surrounds a young woman who has fainted.

A WOMAN IN THE CROWD: Poor thing! Look at her. She has a little baby in her arms too. It was lucky I saw her or she would have fallen and hurt herself.

MAN: (*comes up*) What is it? What has happened?

ONE FROM THE CROWD: Looks as if she's come to get some medicine. Must have fainted.

AN ACTOR: There she's regaining consciousness now.

WOMAN: (*stands up with difficulty*) Where is my child?

WOMAN IN THE CROWD: She's here … She's here … Don't be upset. Have you come from very far, daughter?

WOMAN: A distance of 50 cents on the bus.

ANOTHER FROM THE CROWD: With whom did you come?

WOMAN: I came alone.

FROM THE CROWD: What with this little infant in arms! You should have come with someone. How will you get back?

WOMAN: I'll rest a little and then go.

CROWD: Well, we must be leaving. Visiting hours will soon be over.

They move away in ones and twos. Only the man and woman are left on stage.

MAN: What a crazy thing to do. To come alone when you are so sick!

WOMAN: Who is there to accompany me sir? (*She looks away, sadly.*)

MAN: Forgive me. I asked without knowing. How will you get back now?

WOMAN: I'll stay awhile and go when I feel stronger. I was probably faint from hunger. I have not eaten for several days because of the fever.

MAN: Wait a moment. I'll get you something to drink.

WOMAN: No … No … It doesn't matter.

The man turns and leaves. When he reaches center stage, the entire stage goes dark once more. The light falls only on his face.

MAN: That was a very strange day. I was filled with an overwhelming compassion for her. I gave her something to drink and saw her to her home. I can't think why I felt so sorry for her. Four days later I went to see her again.

As this speech ends a doorway appears behind him (i.e. actors bring in a simple door frame). He goes to the door. At the same moment, another man walks out of the door, glances knowingly at him and walks on. The man pauses awhile thinking, then knocks.

WOMAN: (*from within*) Who is it that knocks like a first-timer? Walk in, there's no one here now.

MAN: It's me.

The Woman opens the door.

WOMAN: Oh sir … forgive me! … I thought sir … Do come in …

The Man enters.

Sit down, sir. I don't know how to thank you, sir. I couldn't even show my gratitude the other day.

MAN: Where is your child?

WOMAN: Asleep.

MAN: Is there anyone else in the house?

WOMAN: No, just my child and me. There is no one else.

MAN: Don't be angry for asking, but where is the child's father?

WOMAN: Why ask such unnecessary questions?

MAN: The other day, seeing you in that state I was filled with a strange compassion. That's why I came back to see you. That's why I'm asking these questions.

WOMAN: Don't ask me about that, sir. It is not the kind of pleasant story you want to talk about.

MAN: You keep it all inside and suffer in silence.

WOMAN: The grief is mine alone. What is the good of talking about it?

MAN: One must talk about it to know whether it will do one good or not. Otherwise, how can one tell? When a person suffers grief or a loss one must share it with someone else. Otherwise, by keeping it bottled up inside, one ends up mad and bitter with the world.

WOMAN: I haven't even bitterness left any more. No. The only thing left in my heart is the desire to keep my child alive.

MAN: That's the very reason I asked the question. I'm not trying to get pleasure out of finding out something you don't want to talk about. But my heart tells me I can do something to help you. Knowing that possibility it would shame my humanity to look on and do nothing.

WOMAN: (*To herself*) Is this yet another devil seeking to make a prey of me? At first every fellow says the same thing. But once they realize your poverty and vulnerability they turn it to their advantage. Then I become merely the object of their lust—a toy. The filthy pigs …!

MAN: Why are you brooding? Am I in the way?

WOMAN: Well, you may as well hear this and be moved. But I tell you sir, I don't need your pity.

She walks to the center stage. The lights dim and only her face is lit. She sings:

I was bound to him by love
Love that knows no bounds
I loved him like my life
Made him my god.

ACTORS IN CHORUS:

Nothing in the world brings more pleasure
Than love and its happiness.

WOMAN:

One dark and rainy evening
He accepted my chaste love
Each day dragged me to ruin
Mind and body all his.

Then one day I said to my lover,
"Dear one, I am with child"

Everything changed in that instant
And our fond dream world died.

Gardens turned to deserts
In my cloud-filled mind.
He said he loved me but left me,
Now I am alone.

As she sings an actor and actress dance on one side of the stage. It is western style waltz.

WOMAN: To this day I have not set eyes on him. I looked for him everywhere. All he had told me were lies.

The dancing pair of actors continue to dance.

DIRECTOR: (*to the dancers*) Here … here … stop that dancing you two! (*to the Woman*) You, go on with your story.

WOMAN: I lost my father when we were still children. Our mother looked after us. When she learned of my problem she did all she could, but she wasted away before our very eyes, consumed by an inner grief. She died not long after the child was born. My brothers and sisters blamed me. Said I had killed her and drove me out of the house.

MAN: Then whose is this little place?

WOMAN: We pay rent and live in it, my child and I.

MAN: Have you no relatives?

WOMAN: They've all deserted me saying I was a loose woman.

MAN: With no one to support you and without a job, how do you and your child manage to live?

One of the actors seated on stage stands up.

ACTOR: Ha … ha … what a joke! There's a stork. "Is that stork white?" he asks! This man asks this woman how she earns a living when it's all there, laid out before his very eyes! What man, didn't you see that fellow come out even as you came in? Doesn't it click even now?

MAN: I know, I know. I understand. What I wanted was to hear it from her.

ACTOR: Well, the truth is the truth, no matter from whom you hear it.

MAN: No, it does matter. She will then understand that she's fallen to the furthest depth that any human being can go.

ACTOR: What good does that do you, her understanding that?

MAN: If she understands herself then it will be very easy for her to understand me.

DIRECTOR: Well, did you hear it from her?

MAN: Yes, after two or three days of questioning she told me all about herself. But she will not accept that what she does is wrong.

WOMAN: (*singing*)

I won't give bloody death a victim
I will protect my little one.
To keep him alive I too must live
Whatever I do in that just cause
Cannot be wrong.

MAN: Your goal is just and what you do may not be wrong, but you are young and strong. You can surely find a better form of employment to keep alive.

WOMAN: Employment! Ha! Who will give a woman like me a job? I looked everywhere for employment. The only job I got from them was this job.

MAN: I don't think it's too late for you to begin a new life.

WOMAN: How can I? The man I loved destroyed my life, and having committed such a serious crime, he just disappeared.

MAN: If all men were kind and caring, this earth would be a far happier place. But there must be someone—some man who can love you truly and honestly.

WOMAN: I don't need either love or pity now. All I want is to keep my child alive. For that I must keep alive. To live, one needs money. I do this for the money. That's all.

MAN: Can one live for money alone? How can you live like that for ever? Alone? Loneliness can be depressing, miserable, deadly. It is a frightening thing.

WOMAN: Sir, why do you harass me with such talk?

MAN: See! You are afraid of loneliness. Everyone fears loneliness. Man is born alone, dies alone, but he cannot live alone. We live with others in a society. You will do whatever you must to survive but that is not living. A person must have some goal to live for and there must be a meaning to life. Society will not condone the life you now lead.

WOMAN: Society? Who or what is society? Society is men! It is they who abandoned me with a child. It is they who drove me out of my home. It is they who showed me the way to this form of employment.

MAN: You say all this because you really don't know men. People make mistakes. People are cheated, taken in. But one must rectify those mistakes. It is hard, I admit. But you don't have to fall to such depths and live alone. Don't you want a stable life with a husband and children?

WOMAN: Why not? Who wouldn't like such a life? Isn't that every woman's dream? But for me it is only a dream.

MAN: All our hopes and wishes are only dreams. So long as they remain hopes they are only dreams. But if we try hard enough we can free ourselves of that dream world and fully awakened make a reality of it. What we need is a clear goal and a firm commitment.

WOMAN: Sir, what nonsense you talk!

MAN: I can give you a better life than this. I promise you that.

WOMAN: Don't talk of such fairy-tale worlds. In the past others have also conjured up dream worlds for me. They lasted only till their own needs were satisfied. Then they left, like dogs who sleep in ditches and when the sun comes up start their aimless loafing again. If sir, you have any desires that need to be satisfied, you may do so and leave. I don't even want the money.

MAN: If that was all I wanted I wouldn't have hung around you so long like this. I sincerely love you. Can't you believe me?

WOMAN: It's not that I can't believe you. But I'm a woman who has been burned with a blazing firebrand. Now I fear even a firefly.

MAN: But you are living in the midst of flames.

WOMAN: If so, I'm the only one who burns. I don't need to drag others into it.

MAN: I want to pull you out of that fire.

WOMAN: I'm an abandoned woman with a child. You are still young. Go find yourself a beautiful bride.

MAN: *(to himself)* Why do I run after this vagrant woman? Do I really love her or do I not? Can I leave her to destroy herself in this way and just look on? Why doesn't she realize what she is doing? How these women destroy their lives! Why don't they do something to save themselves? (aloud) What an unfortunate creature I am!

WOMAN: Sir, how can you be more unfortunate than me?

MAN: When one loves sincerely and that love is not accepted, there is no misfortune greater than that.

WOMAN: Sir, you may love me, but it is unlikely that I can love you in return.

MAN: The greatest affection you can show me is merely to live a good life. If you give up this way of life—do just that—it is more than enough for me.

WOMAN: I don't want to lie to you just to have you feed me and support me. Whatever you want, at whatever time, you are free to come to me. Let us leave it that way. It is the only thing I can do to repay your kindness.

She walks up to him and embraces him. He pushes her away roughly.

MAN: Get away from me. I didn't come to you for that. If that was all I wanted there are many other places I could go.

WOMAN: *(angry)* In that case, go! What the hell did you come creeping in here for? It is because you helped me on that one occasion that I'm checking myself and being polite. Now, get out of my house. If you don't, I'll scream. You know what will happen to you if the denizens of these slums come in here. Therefore, leave.

The man walks around the room, looking about him.

There is nothing more to see. Get out!

DIRECTOR: *(to actors)* The door! Bring back that door …!

At that, two actors bring in the doorway through which he first entered. The man steps out.

2ND ACTOR: Pity you had to get thrown out. Just tell that woman to go to hell and you go about your business.

MAN: I want to save that woman from this hell. I want to show her that there is a better life than this.

1ST ACTOR: Your intentions are fair enough, that is if you can support her and her child.

MAN: I will do so in whatever way I can.

1ST ACTOR: What's your job?

MAN: I don't have a permanent job.

2ND ACTOR: Does that mean that you have a temporary job?

MAN: For men like us everything is temporary. Life itself is impermanent.

1ST ACTOR: But what is it you do?

MAN: I write.

2ND ACTOR: What? Letters?

MAN: No. Books. I write articles for journals and newspapers.

2ND ACTOR: About what or whom?

MAN: About us. About you. About the dreams of that woman and her child and a thousand others like her, who suffer from injustice. About a world free of exploiters.

1ST ACTOR: What! You have written so much and haven't become famous yet? You are hardly known. The first thing you have to do, man, is make a name for yourself. Then people will accept whatever you write.

MAN: I wrote two books. Both were banned.

2ND ACTOR: Why? Were they pornography?

MAN: They must have seemed obscene to those who banned them.

1ST ACTOR: Was it after that that you abandoned writing and took this job?

MAN: What job?

DIRECTOR: (*cuts in*) Hm … Hm … When we began this production wasn't it the woman who ran in saying you were chasing her to kill her. Now it seems that it was she who chased you out of her house.

MAN: Don't get it mixed up. What you saw just now was what happened three years ago.

1ST ACTRESS: Oh Lord! Do we have to sit through three more years of this!

DIRECTOR: Look here! Be patient. Now tell us what happened after that?

MAN: About two or three days later I went again to see her.

The doorway appears once more. The man knocks. The woman opens the door. The man walks in talking to the actors seated on either side of the stage.

I was met with a warmer welcome on that occasion. I explained everything to her. What my goals and ideals were. What was important about our coming together. What special help she could give me in my work. I told her too about the book I was writing.

WOMAN: (*pointing to a book on a table*) There, that's me on the cover!

MAN: Unfortunately, no one is likely to look at it.

WOMAN: Don't be afraid. With a woman on the cover they are not likely to ban it.

MAN: It's not just the cover. The whole book is about the thousands of other sufferers like you. Every word is filled with our pain, with our sighs, with our dreams. If I'm to finish it, we must be together. Work on it together.

WOMAN: Oh no. What do I understand of all that?

MAN: You may not understand at first, but you will later. A day will come when all men will understand. Only with your help can I complete this book. But during that short time, you will have to bear with me patiently.

WOMAN: As if my life till now has been without suffering. I'm prepared for anything so long as it does not hurt my child. I'm ready for anything. I've lived only for my child. Now you must be a good father to him.

MAN: No, no! Are you mad!

WOMAN: Why do you say that now?

MAN: I said that because we haven't begun to live together yet. Before I become a father to your child, I must be your man. (*They embrace.*)

1ST ACTOR: Hurray! A celebration! Let's have a party.

The cast enact a mock wedding, sing songs and dance drunkenly. When the song is over they leave. There is a light cut. When the lights come on again only the man and woman are on stage. The woman is now very pregnant.

MAN: The section I wrote today is fantastic. Listen: "The entire sky is filled with poisonous fumes and the world is stricken by the fierce rays of the devil sun that settles on it. Our world will die before long. The rays of heat come through a white, clear, empty, sky. They fall on us, destroy us. The sky fills with poisoned fumes."

WOMAN: I suppose all we can do then is to go up in smoke!

MAN: There, you've ruined it! I was just beginning to spell it out beautifully. You never allow me to finish.

WOMAN: By the time you finish that book we'll all be finished! Dead!

MAN: Why do you always make such unfortunate comments? All our destinies hang on this book of mine. The world waits expectantly for it. I'm now fairly near the end. When the rest is done we can live happily. Our child that is soon to be born can grow up strong, get a good education, and when he grows up, find employment to suit his talents. We and everyone else can live without this constant fear of starvation and death. But before we achieve all that we must finish this book.

WOMAN: Nothing will come of all that useless talk. Do some kind of a job and try to earn something—anything.

MAN: I cannot sell my soul for money. I have an enormous responsibility to fulfill, before I can earn money.

WOMAN: You wrote and wrote till you nearly died and twice your books were banned. The same fate will happen to this one too.

MAN: No, it won't happen. I will not let it happen. If that happens the sighs and sorrows of the downtrodden who suffer will turn each and every letter into thunderbolts and strike the rotten world and smash it to pieces. Thereafter, a new world free of corruption and terror, where new men with new ideas can live again, will be established. The beautiful world we hope for is not too far away.

WOMAN: Women who are pregnant should eat well. They must have a lot of rest. The doctor said I was too anemic and wanted me to take some pills.

MAN: OK, OK. I told you I would get them for you in a day or two.

WOMAN: Ha! From the day we began living together you've been bringing things! Don't give me that talk.

MAN: If it's not me, who is it who provides you with even one meal every other day?

WOMAN: There were many others who would have brought me meals if you hadn't taken to living here.

MAN: What did you say? Instead of sleeping around with each and every man how much more dignified is the life you lead now? At least you now have a man you can call your own who loves you. Can't you take any pleasure in that?

WOMAN: Yes, I may take pleasure in that. But can this older child of mine and this one in my womb get any pleasure from it? I've had enough of your beggarly bodhisattva talk!

MAN: There's a limit to my patience. Shut that mouth of yours!

WOMAN: I've shut up long enough. Until this fool's ridiculous world is realized do I and my child not have to live? It will happen today. It will work out tomorrow, I thought and waited. You didn't let me mind my own business and bring up my child as best as I knew. Now, I have an added burden.

MAN: Can a child be a burden to its mother? A country's future is its children.

ACTORS: (*chant*) Those who are motherly, may they have children
Those who love farming, may they have land!

WOMAN: What ridiculous nonsense!

1ST ACTRESS: How will she feed them without a man to support her?

MAN: I told you not to talk about our personal affairs with all and sundry and shame me in the eyes of the world.

WOMAN: If you have such a desire for respectability, why did you come to roost here in these gutters and alley-ways?

MAN: What? What did you say?

The man glares angrily at the woman, grabs the books and papers he's been working on, flings them on the floor and is about to walk off stage.

DIRECTOR: Stop, stop. Where are you off to?

MAN: No, I can't perform in this way. These people will never understand me.

DIRECTOR: (*stopping him*) But you can't leave in the middle of the scene like this! Think about your child, your unborn child, a new generation.

MAN: It was for them that I worked so hard.

1ST ACTOR: If you slip off now what will be their fate? Is there any sense in you leaving them and then saying you did all this for their sake?

MAN: I, too, don't want to destroy everything.

1ST ACTOR: You struggled so hard to get her to accept you. In spite of so many differences you two were able to come together. The result of that union is the child that is yet to be born. Did you work so hard just to produce yet another orphan? You are that child's hope.

DIRECTOR: Yes, yes, you are that unborn child's only hope.

MAN: You are right, I'm his one hope. I know that. I cannot run away from that responsibility. If I do, even that unborn child will curse me. I will return to her. (*The man goes back.*)

MAN: (*Seven months later. The man is returning home at the end of the day.*) If those around me had not talked me into going back this story might have been different. I returned determined that, in spite of whatever problems arose, I would not turn away without finishing my book. It is now seven months since our child was born. The peace and quiet necessary for my work is gone. In any case, it is not the kind of book one can write by sticking inside the house. So, I leave early in the morning, spend the entire day engaged in my work and come home exhausted only to sleep. This morning, too, I left early and returned home only about an hour ago.

The doorway appears again. The man goes to the door. The same scene that took place in the first act is now repeated. The man knocks at the door. The woman speaks from within.

WOMAN: Who is it, knocking at my door like a first timer? Walk in, there's no one here now.

MAN: It's me.

The woman opens the door. The man enters.

Have you gone back to your filthy job again? Can't you be patient for a little longer?

WOMAN: Filthy job? You, too, have eaten from those earnings these past months.

MAN: Why do you deceive me like this?

WOMAN: You have no right to question me. You are not my legal husband.

MAN: But you are now the mother of my child.

WOMAN: That was not of my seeking or for my pleasure. It was not I who went after you. You are the one who came here groveling on your knees.

MAN: You … you liked it. You agreed to help me—to live with me.

WOMAN: Yes, I agreed, reluctantly.

MAN: Then you lived all this time with me reluctantly, disliking it?

WOMAN: I did not live with you. You lived with me.

MAN: You bloody bitch! Whore!

He strides threateningly towards her. She screams in fear. He grabs her and tries to slap her. She slips out of his grasp, grabs her child and runs. It is a replay of the first scene.

MAN: Where are you running? Stop.
WOMAN: No, I won't, I won't. I don't want to be killed for no fault of mine.
MAN: I, too, don't want to be a murderer for no fault of mine. Let's go back home.
WOMAN: Leave me to lead my own life and you go worship at any shrine you wish.
MAN: Whatever shrine I worship at I now can't leave you.
WOMAN: You should have thought of that before begetting a child.
MAN: I can't waste time talking to you here in this place. Come on let's go home.
WOMAN: No I won't go.

They struggle. The actors jump in and break up the fight.

3RD ACTOR: Tough one that. She deserves to be beaten up.
2ND ACTOR: That's the way with these women. They are all deceiving whores.
1ST ACTRESS: Strange woman, to talk to her man like that!
2ND ACTRESS: Ultimately it's the children who suffer because of adults' fights.
2ND ACTOR: I don't know why they bring children into this world if it is to abandon them. They must know to act according to their means.
1ST ACTOR: Then, is it only the rich who should have children? If that were the rule my friend, neither you nor I would be around today!
1ST ACTRESS: You can discuss such theoretical questions later. Kindly solve the problem we now have on our hands.
DIRECTOR: We now understand the problem. We said we would help in whatever way we could. Think about it all of you and come up with suggestions as to what we should do.
3RD ACTOR: The one thing left is to hand them both over to the police.
2ND ACTOR: Much good the police would do. Have they ever solved anything yet?
MAN: I told you our story because I had faith that you would look at this matter intelligently.
DIRECTOR: We understand. We have not broken your trust. We will come up with a solution. Just give us a little time to think of something and meanwhile you two stop your squabbling.
1ST ACTOR: Hurray! A ceasefire!
DIRECTOR: That's very dangerous. Most crimes are committed during a ceasefire. Let's drop the 'fire' and just 'cease' for a moment and let's all take a short break.

Interval

As the curtain opens the actors are getting into costume. The Man and Woman come up on stage.

DIRECTOR: Our troupe came up with several different ideas, some quite good but a little impractical. To tell you the truth we can't provide a definite solution to your problem. We are only actors. But it is our duty to show you possible solutions. Let's go to Buddhist history for an illustration. We all know the story of the Buddha in his earlier life as King Vessantara and of his queen, Madri. That was the best example we could think of. We have decided to perform it for your benefit. The cast is now getting ready. You two sit here and watch the performance. (*To the actors*) Are you ready over there?

ACTORS: Yes, we are ready.

To a background music of drums the actors dance in a circle and sit on a side like the chorus in a traditional stylized or ritual dramatic performance. One of them comes forward as the story-teller.

STORYTELLER:

Like a moon amid stars here comes queen Madri attended by her children. Loving, determined, see how she follows her banished lord. Here is queen Madri in the Vangagiri forest.
Look on wide eyed. See how her presence lights up this stage!

Queen Madri enters and dances in a circle to the beat of drums and sings.

I cannot live without my husband, lord,
I cannot stay without my moon-like lord,
How will you live in that wild forest, lord?
Who'll see to your needs, alone in the wilderness?

She bows her head and weeps. King Vessantara enters.

VESSANTARA: Don't grieve my queen. Our one aim, yours and mine, was to work for the welfare of our people. But they are dissatisfied and have had the great King Sanda banish me to the Vangagiri forest. I am not angry with them. My compassionate concern for them will always remain. I will now go to Vangagiri and strive to achieve my goal.

MADRI: (*singing*)

A river without water is empty, exposed.
A land without a king is equally exposed.
A woman without a husband is naked, exposed.
However hard the forest life, I will follow you.

VESSANTARA: I fear your coming may be an obstacle to my attaining my goal of Buddhahood. I must go alone.

MADRI: My lord, you are not used to forest life. What joy is there away from all human company?

VESSANTARA:

Gem studded palaces
Ambrosial foods
Pleasures of the flesh
What use?
All around I see
only darkness and grief.
You stay with the children.
As for me,
I must go forth
Alone.

MADRI: Stay lord. I would rather follow you to the ends of the earth than face the grief of separation.

She falls on her knees before the king.

STORYTELLER: The queen now lives in the forest with her husband and their two children. She serves her hermit husband in whatever way she can; scours the forest for sweet fruits to keep her children alive and works unceasingly so her husband can achieve his goal of Buddhahood.

The dance troupe finish their performance and bow to the audience.

DIRECTOR: We were not interested in King Vessantara's goals or his ascetic practices. What we wanted was to show this woman Queen Madri's character. Vessantara was able to become a Buddha only because of a woman like her.

2ND ACTOR: The Queen never said a word against him, not even when he gave away his children to that old devil Jūjaka.[1]

WOMAN: I'm not so foolish as to give away my children to a Jujaka. However, if there is a King Vessantara around I'll gladly give him my children. At least they will get enough to eat and drink then!

2ND ACTOR: Vessantara gave away his children in order to become a Buddha.

WOMAN: Oh yes, this man here too may become a Buddha, but after that what? My children and I will be left to beg in the streets.

2ND ACTOR: Well, there are other forms of enlightenment to strive for—Buddhas, Pachcheka Buddhas, sovans, sakadagamins,[2] a whole string of other categories.

WOMAN: There's plenty of time to become a Buddha in another life. First one must do something to survive in this life.

1ST ACTOR: You know, there are some Buddhist texts that say it doesn't matter what one does to survive. The important thing according to them is to keep a serene mind at the moment of death. Then pst … no problem … its straight to heaven with no further talk!

DIRECTOR: This is no time to joke. Stop laughing. We may all have to cry soon.

2ND ACTRESS: It is a joke! A woman must go through hell so a man can go off alone and become a Buddha!

MAN: I have no desire to go off alone and become a Buddha. I want us all to become Buddhas. I don't have Vessantara's madness. Nor do I have inherited wealth to give away like he did. All I'm saying is that in order to save the lives of thousands of children, our children will have to suffer a little. That can't be helped.

WOMAN: Why should my children suffer for the sake of others?

MAN: We must consider every child our own. If all men thought as you did we would still be living in caves.

WOMAN: Sure! These are heavenly abodes that we happen to be living in now! Buddhas or no Buddhas what good does it do us? The gods only favor the criminals.

MAN: The biggest crime we commit is to look on and do nothing—leaving the criminal to the care of the gods!

WOMAN: I lived a free life, not beholden to anyone. You ruined my life. Is that not a crime?

Unable to respond the man looks down and is silent. The actors now become singers and sing on his behalf.

ACTORS: (*singing*)

Understand. Comprehend. Ask the questions
Who am I? What has happened to me?
You will know then
A sea-change has occurred.

WOMAN: He writes about this man and that man, but what good has it ever been to us?

ACTORS: (*singing*)

Many are the heroes
who give their lives
to save others
forced to suffer.
We must protect them
we must support them
sacrifice ourselves
if the need arises.

WOMAN: I have no life left to sacrifice for such things.

1ST ACTOR: Don't be short-sighted. Look ahead to the future.

WOMAN: I have no time to look ahead or behind. Once these little ones are old enough to fend for themselves I won't live a moment longer suffering like this.

1ST ACTOR: Dying is not a solution. One must live. You, your children, we must all live.

2ND ACTOR: What are you up to now man? Are you now trying to take on this piece of baggage?

1ST ACTOR: That's not the question. We've already taken it on. How can we dismiss it as only that man's problem? It is everybody's problem.

2ND ACTOR: How's that? We were engaged in a performance. This woman crashed in here. That doesn't make her our problem.

The actors discuss the issue hotly. They are clearly on two sides now. The Director tries to make peace. To the Woman

DIRECTOR: Why can't you understand? We've taken such pains to make you see.

WOMAN: Why does everyone blame me? Didn't I suffer in silence all these months? One fellow left me pregnant, abandoned me and ran away. Another promised me kingly comforts but what did I get? Nothing! If we ate one meal, we starved all next day. No money for an illness, for essential medicines. The child's schooling had to stop. To add to everything, I now have to cope with his temper and fear for my life. I'm worse off than I was. That's the only difference.

1ST ACTRESS: Oh, but there is another difference—a very clear difference. This man did not exploit you and abandon you. He promises to make your life happier.

WOMAN: Promises! I've heard them till I'm sick!

DIRECTOR: The situation where you allowed others to dictate to you has now changed. The time has come for a momentous decision. Think of all the long-term implications before you decide. Everything depends on your decision.

WOMAN: What's so important about my decision?

1ST ACTOR: The most valuable thing in life is what one creates oneself. The farmer, the worker, the scientist, the artist, the revolutionary, even mothers, each create something new for the world.

DIRECTOR: None of those things are the creation of any one individual. They require a community, a sense of unity.

WOMAN: I don't understand all that mumbo jumbo. Not one thing! All I want is to bring up my children and live free. Oh, you gods, what have I done to suffer like this?

She hugs her child and falls to her knees. The actors look on silently for a few moments.

DIRECTOR: (*to the Man*) Well, we tried our best to make her see reason. There's nothing more we can do.

1ST ACTOR: (*to the Director*) Can you slip out of it so easily? What about the confidence he placed in us? What about our promise to her?

DIRECTOR: I've kept my promise. There's nothing more I can do.

He is fed up, marches to the far side of the stage and sits down. Some of the actors follow and sit beside him. Other actors look on and laugh at him.

2ND ACTOR: If it's reached the point when even the fence and the hedge have begun to eat the grain, why then I'll join in and eat some too![3]

He joins the Director's group.

MAN: All you people are like rice seedlings growing in a small field. From the time I was young I saw how fences and hedges meant to protect the grain swallowed it up instead. It happened before my eyes and I didn't know whom to tell or what to do. Everyone shut their eyes consciously or unconsciously, and allowed it to happen. Must it always happen so, I asked myself? I sought everywhere for an answer. This woman is one rice plant in that field among a hundred thousand others. They are all trapped between the fence and the hedge and so don't understand me. They won't even try to understand. Even when they do understand they do nothing. What is left for us when both the fence and hedge eat up the paddy plants in this way? Can I, too, look on as if I were deaf and dumb? This is a terrible crime, an injustice.

The Sponsor, who, up to now, had sat silently in the auditorium enters with two security guards.

SPONSOR: (*to the actors*) Look here you people—what are you waiting for? Can't you hear the mumbo-jumbo this madman is mouthing? It's a sickness, a disease one can't ignore. If he was just an ordinary man who lived for the day, aware of the certainty of death, it would not matter. But this devil is not normal. He is abnormal. To be abnormal is to be sick.

GUARD: I think its a form of demonic possession and that's not easy to cure.

SPONSOR: If he is possessed then we must exorcise the demon in him and make him a normal man again.

2ND GUARD: Sure. That's easy enough! What we have to do is perform a mini exorcist ritual and offer a sacrifice to the demon.

SPONSOR: Then will the demon who has taken possession of this man accept the sacrifice and leave quietly without troubling us any more.

1ST ACTOR: What? Do we now have to perform an exorcistic ceremony too? But more important than driving the demon from this man, is to rid this land of all the curses that roost here.

SPONSOR: Look here, look here, Mr. Director. You had better remind your actors that this show was organized with my money. You took an advance from me not to put on this crazy performance. If you don't put on the show I want, you will have to reimburse me for all I've spent so far.

DIRECTOR: Please be patient. There's a big problem here.

SPONSOR: I gave you more than enough time. Now I've come to solve this big problem, which you couldn't solve, and I'll do it my way. Look here you—you fellow. If you are mad, go to a mental hospital. You come here and upset all our work. I've waited long enough. There's a limit to my patience.

MAN: You believe that anyone who doesn't think like you is mad. I, too, have been patient long enough. I've suffered insults and abuse. I put up with all this to achieve my goal of a better world, to give this woman a better life. But that has become a joke to her. Now I've become a joke to all of you too—a madman, a lunatic! Tell me, can a man take any more of this?

He walks up to the Sponsor and grabs him by the throat. Sponsor wriggles out of his grasp and runs to a corner of the stage.

SPONSOR: Was I wrong when I said the man was mad, possessed? He's a demon. (*to the guards*) What are you waiting for? Hurry up. Begin the exorcist ceremony.[4]
The guards begin chanting like ritual priests.

We take refuge in the Great Jeweled Buddha,
We take refuge in his Doctrine and his monks,
We take refuge in these three great Jewels.[5]

Oh gods of Sun and Moon,
Goddess of Earth,
All ye great gods
Grant us your powers!

The guards dance around the man and prepare to beat him, with strands of coconut or arecanut flowers, just as ritual specialists beat their patients during an exorcism.

TROUPE:

In the world's four corners
The fire-gods dwell
Out of the fire's furor
Dust-clouds swell.

SPONSOR:

Fire-demons do not terrify this patient
Use your powers, cure him oh ye gods!

TROUPE:

Mounds of skeletons appear[6]
Graves sprout along the roads.

SPONSOR:

Fire and destruction strike the ear
By your powers cure him oh ye gods!

TROUPE:

From beyond the seas they come, the demons vile,
They leap and play in lonely resting places

SPONSOR:

Money and silks as offerings they provide.
By your powers cure him oh ye gods!

TROUPE:

The fires of hunger burn fierce and bright
Wives are sent to far off lands as sacrifice[7]

SPONSOR:

Bring the goddess of wealth by airplane to your abode.
Cure him by your powers you powerful gods!

TROUPE:

Empty heads have risen to high places
While heads of innocents roll and burn in fires

SPONSOR:

Guardian gods must come to protect all creatures
May the land and the language be blessed oh ye gods!

As the exorcism ends the man falls exhausted in a faint as patients do in such rituals. The actors stand back. The guards encircle him and dance chanting:

GUARDS: All you beings who are in possession of this patient, demons, devils, ghosts, madmen, accept this ritual sacrifice we offer and depart to the far corners of the universe. May we live a hundred thousand years, free of pain, grief, and disease, have land and wealth, houses and goods, cars and vans, high office and status, and shine in splendor with royal, regal, power. In that hope and believing in that good fortune may all sorrow and the darkness of disease be gone from him, all ended, finished!

The guards get chains. The Sponsor comes up to the fallen man, puts the chains round his neck and tries to drag him off.

SPONSOR: It's all done and over with now—the big problem that you fellows took so long and couldn't solve. We live in an atmosphere of law and order. Now that things are quiet and peaceful hurry up and begin your performance.

MAN: No, I won't be shamefully docile like this. I underwent so much hardship and suffering for so long not to end like this. Can you fellows not think of a better ending than this rotten acceptance?[8]

SPONSOR: That's the only good and easy solution.

1ST ACTOR: No that's a deception. That's a crime that will go down in history. Knowing what is right and what should be done can we permit such things to happen? (*to the woman*) Why don't you live with him for a short while and help him to achieve his goal? Alternatively, man, give up your high-faluting ideas and do something, anything, any kind of a job. But, of course, she won't do the one and he won't do the other.

2ND ACTOR: It is not as easy as one imagines to get two people to agree to accept a single goal and be committed to it. That's what this man hopes to do with our help.

DIRECTOR: But that's what we've been trying to do all this time. We even stopped our performance for it.

2ND ACTOR: But we found no solution. The problem still exists, and we are not any further along. Our performance has stopped. Everything is in mad confusion. (*to the Man*) What more do you want from us? Are you asking us to die for your cause?

MAN: There's no need to die. No need to mess up your performance either. My patience, too, is at an end. You may think me a criminal but there's nothing else I can do. In order to make this woman accept my goals I must do this.

He goes to the Woman and tries to drag her out with him.

This may not be your legal husband talking but it is the man who loves you and is the father of your child. I want to live with you because I don't wish to make that child also a fatherless orphan. Let us live like human beings or let us die. That's better than living like dogs. Today we must choose one or the other. Until my book is completed we will all have to suffer for just a while longer. You should put up with this and be a little patient. This is the last time I'll ask you. Answer me in one word. Can you or can't you?

The woman shakes him off, looks at the man a long time. Then without a word she gets down from the stage and leaves the hall with her child. The man hesitates, seems confused, and follows slowly after. The actors, too, are about to follow but they hear the theme music of their performance. They listen for a moment as if about to go back on stage, and then, one by one, they too leave the stage. The Director and Sponsor find the actors all gone, give up, shrug their shoulders, and leave. Only the ushers\guards are left. They look about them unsure and are about to follow when the curtain falls rapidly and cuts them off on stage.

The end

****

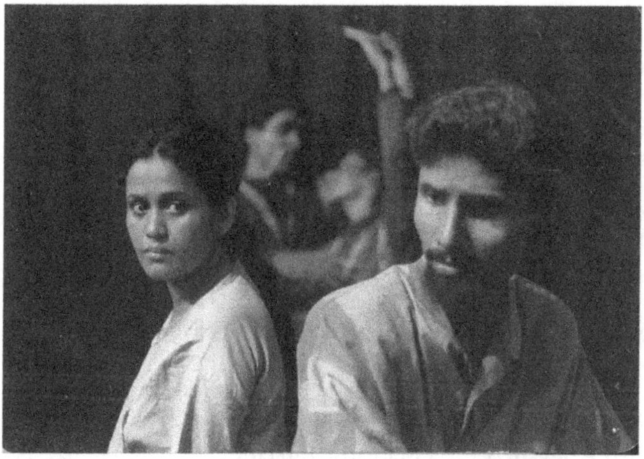

PHOTOGRAPH 2.1 The Man and the Woman in *The Bearer of Woes*. Photograph by Sarath Meddaduwa

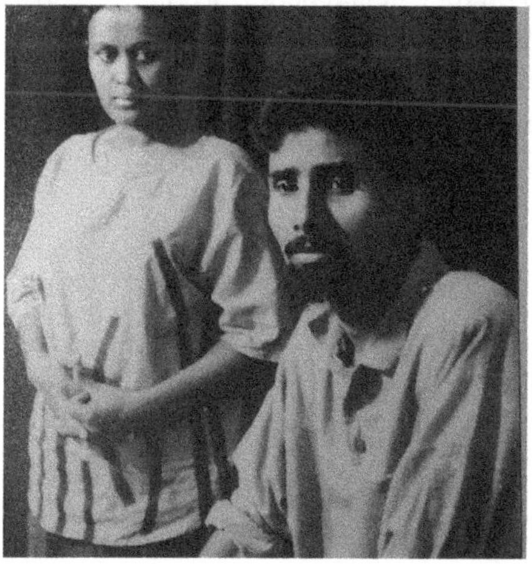

PHOTOGRAPH 2.2 The Man and the Woman in *The Bearer of Woes*. Photograph by Sarath Meddaduwa

Notes

1 Jūjaka is a Brahmin beggar who asks Vessantara for his two children. Vessantara, who has given away all his possessions, gifts his children, too, to Jūjaka.
2 These were followers of the Buddhist Doctrine who achieved different stages in the path to Enlightenment.
3 A popular saying implying: When those who are supposed to provide security are themselves involved in the acts of violation, then the only thing left to do is to join in and do the same. In this case the Director who was supposed to try and solve the problem is opting out. So others follow suit.
4 Exorcist ceremonies are ritual performances intended to cure psychological illnesses seen also as demonic possessions in the culture. They can be cured by exorcising the demon that is causing the psychological depression or manic state, by performing specific rituals.
5 Initial verses of a standard invocation to the Buddha.
6 A reference to the mass killings of young people suspected of belonging to the JVP revolutionary movement, by police and government sponsored para-military personnel during the late 1980s. This play was written during that time and the author was a young man of 25.
7 During this period, women in large numbers went to the Middle East to work as domestics, often encouraged by their husbands to go. They lived and worked for the most part under appalling conditions—almost like indentured labor. But in spite of the horror stories that from time to time were highlighted in the press, employment conditions in Sri Lanka were so bad that hundreds of thousands continued to go.
8 "Acceptance" here would mean to go back to square one: leave the woman to her earlier way of earning a living and he to give up on his dream to change the world with his writings. It could also mean accepting life as it is and continue without questioning.

***

Prasannajith Abeysuriya is a dramatist, director and actor. He has spent the better part of his life in the theater. Now a lecturer in the University of Fine Arts Colombo, he has extended his world into teaching students, introducing them into the excitement and challenges of the theater world. A versatile actor, a familiar figure both on stage and on film, he has performed in the works of many of his fellow dramatists and directors. He began acting with the Wayside and Open Street Theatre group under the brilliant direction of Gamini Haththotuwegama where many of the best actors of the day cut their teeth. Prasannajith himself writes and produces for the theater as was the case with *Dukgannarala* in 1993 and *Doradanda* in 1995, which have won national awards.

THE JURY (JŪRIYA 1993)

Dhananjaya Karunarathne

Characters

MANUVANSA—A man about 35 years old. He is in a pair of oversized shorts that fall below his knees, a loose dark tee shirt and a pair of old shoes.

BUNJĀ and BAHITĒ—Two garbage collectors, about 40 years old, working for the town council. They too wear oversized shorts like Manuvansa, tattered tee shirts and worn-out old shoes.

HENCHARĀLA—The chief security officer. He has an enormous beard and belly and is about 50 years old. He wears a khaki uniform with long sleeves and long pants; he has on a cap and shoes.

TWO JUNIOR OFFICERS (CLERKS)—They wear khaki outfits with short sleeves and short pants and shoes.

VAHANSĒ (THE REVEREND)—A priest/monk whose specific religious identity is not clear. He is bald. His upper body is clothed in a brown robe and beneath it he wears a pair of large dark pants. His shoes are those of a priest. He is about 65 years old.

THE PETITIONER/COMPLAINANT—A man of about 35 who has recovered from a serious injury. He wears the shirt and pants and shoes of an ordinary lower middle class person.

ENGELSINA—An upper class woman of about 65 years. She is in a caftan generally worn by women of that class in the home, and has on a pair of shoes.

DOG—A feisty handsome dog with an identification tag around his neck.

MANUVANSA'S LAWYER—He wears the tie and coat of a lawyer but his clothes are a trifle worn. He is about 45 years old.

THE JUDGE—He is short. About 65 years. Stammers. Has a spineless look about him. He is dressed in the robes of a judge.

HENCHARĀLA'S LAWYER—He is about 50 years old and wears the slightly worn-out garb of a small-time lawyer.

SUNVUNĀ—Manuvansa's wife, of about 30. She is in a long skirt and blouse and a pair of old shoes. Her clothes reveal she is poor.

THE VETERINARIAN—He is in the doctor's coat of a veterinarian; is fairly short and wears glasses.

TWO COURT OFFICERS—They wear the uniform, hat and shoes of court officials.

THE DOCTOR—Is about 45 years old and has the looks of a drunk. He is thin and wears a doctor's overcoat over his shirt and pants.

Act 1

In the center back of the stage is a stage prop—a wall about a meter thick and two meters high. This remains unchanged from scene to scene but is put to different uses as a wall, a table, etc. As the scenes change the parts are pushed on stage from the two sides, in front of the curtain.

Scene 1: A wall beside a road

Two small pieces of wall appear from either side of the front curtain. Bunjā, Bahitē and Manuvansa enter from the back right of the stage collecting garbage. Bunjā and Bahitē carry the bin, lifting it from each side, while Manuvansa collects the garbage with a shovel and throws it in the bin. Occasionally, he picks up some garbage with his bare hands. Their work is going fairly fast. Bunjā and Bahitē take turns puffing at a beedi[1] *and exhale the smoke. In this manner they move to the right front of the stage.*

BUNJĀ: Manuvansa, so what do you think about your new job?

MANUVANSA: It's good but a little smelly.

BAHITĒ: At first, we also felt that way. After a while, all smells and scents disappear. We picked up this habit of smoking to get over that smell.

MANUVANSA: I was thinking, is there no other use we can make of this waste?

BUNJĀ: Our boss told us the other day that in the developed world they purify even fecal matter and use it again for food. You remember that, Bahitē?

BAHITĒ: Though the man said that I'm glad we are not yet that developed.[2]

MANUVANSA: I don't think we need to develop that much!

BUNJĀ: Don't say that ... They say it's the best way they've discovered to ward off the problem of food shortages for the world. I think they will introduce it to our country too very soon.

BAHITĒ: Yes, that's the only thing we have not yet had to eat!

BUNJĀ: They say it's a modern method. If they give it to us let's just eat it up.

A short silence.

BAHITĒ: Manuvansa you are new. You must be tired. You hold on to this. I will do some shoveling.

MANUVANSA: No, it's not necessary. It's still early in the day so I'm not tired.

BAHITĒ: You seem to me to be a man who hasn't had too hard a time … not been put through the mill …Weren't you married only just recently?

MANUVANSA: Yes.

BAHITĒ: But you seem about 35 years old.

MANUVANSA: Yes, about that.

Manuvansa continues to energetically shovel the garbage. Meanwhile, Bunjā whispers to Bahitē.

BUNJĀ: The man's wife told me yesterday that he was not used to this kind of life. She says we will have to be wary till he gets used to it.

BAHITĒ: How so?

BUNJĀ: He's lived a strange life, not been out much. He was brought up in an orphanage. When he grew up they made a match for him and sent him out here. He has no experience of life outside. The woman is from here. Says he's learned only about good and bad.

BAHITĒ: Manuvansa, couldn't you have looked for a job better suited to your education?

MANUVANSA: Are there such jobs?

Silence. The three of them have now come to the left corner of the stage. As Manuvansa throws a shovelful of dirt over the wall he brings up a man's leg severed at the knee. Manuvansa sees it and is horrified. The other two do not seem bothered at all.

MANUVANSA: It's a leg … a leg … a man's leg. Oh, my good god! What a horrible disaster! A terrible crime has taken place. Don't come near. Keep off. It's a leg. Just look. A man's leg! Oh, my good god it's a newly cut off leg …

Bunjā and Bahitē look at it with mild curiosity but Manuvansa is extremely disturbed and upset. As Bunjā and Bahitē try to get close, Manuvansa raises the shovel in his hand and pushes them back.

Don't come near. Let it be there just as it was.

BAHITĒ: Now … now … Manuvansa. Cool down.

BUNJĀ: Just listen to us a little …

MANUVANSA: (*panting*) Oh my god who has done this horrible crime? Who in heaven's name did this low-down act? Where are the other parts of this man? Why did they throw the leg here? ... I'm shivering … Look, the hair on my body is standing on end. I don't understand ... I don't understand … What should we do now?

BAHITĒ: We will do what has to be done, so move off. You look as if you've seen a ghost … (*Bahitē goes towards the leg.*)

MANUVANSA: Get away from it, man. Let it lie right where it was, or they won't be able to catch the man who committed this low down crime. Don't you fiddle around with this. There has been some major terrible event behind this. Oh my god, I can't bear it. After all, this was a man's life.

BUNJĀ: Stop this shouting. Be quiet and listen to us.

MANUVANSA: Who is in charge of security here? Tell me, where is the security office located? In the name of humanity, we must inform the security post about this. Come with me. Come with me.

BAHITĒ: Man, stop shouting; stop making a fuss. You are like a rabbit that has seen a tiger.

Manuvansa, trembling, pushes the leg with the shovel back where it was and runs out shouting.

BUNJĀ: Wait. Don't run off.

BAHITĒ: Listen to what we tell you, you water buffalo.[3] Stop.

Bahitē and Bunjā run after Manuvansa carrying the bin with them. Manuvansa runs off, shovel in hand.

Scene 2: The security post

As Manuvansa leaves, the stage now turns into a security post. The lighting remains unchanged. The wall at the back center becomes a table. An officer brings a chair from outside and leaves it for a petitioner to sit. The two pieces of wall move out to the sides and are replaced by two pieces of wall with wire netting fixed on them. On one of them is a board that reads "Security Division." On the other is a board that says "In the Service of the Public."

The chief officer, Hencharāla, inquiring into complaints, makes inquiries and using the table makes notes in a book. Two subordinate officers (clerks) help him. Both crowd in on each complainant but one runs out each time an inquiry is over, and runs back as the next one begins. Whatever the nature of the complaint may be, and whether he has work to do or not, one of the two men is a busy body and cannot keep still. The other officer announces the complainants. The complainants come from all over. Vahansē, together with another complainant, comes forward.

JUNIOR OFFICER (CLERK): Next.

HENCHARĀLA: Ah … Vahansē, why is Your Worship here? Have they robbed your temple again?

VAHANSĒ: Thank the gods not yet. But they may do so any day.

He hands over a pistol that he has hidden at his waist. The clerk throws it away and gives him a new one. Vahansē tucks it at his waist.

Recently, they brought a golden image. Since that day I have been suspicious of all who come.

HENCHARĀLA: Next …

COMPLAINANT: Sir, my woman has taken to prostitution. There's nothing I can do to stop her.

HENCHARĀLA: Do you know the places where she hangs out?

COMPLAINANT: I know it only too well … (*looks warily around*). This is what you must do sir. Don't hurt the woman, sir. I care a lot for her. It was only after I was hurt in the bomb attack and bedridden that she perhaps has taken to this kind of work to find the money for my medicines … It's the man with her that you must beat up soundly. Skin him from his eyes down. Then he will lose consciousness.

HENCHARĀLA: That will happen much earlier.

COMPLAINANT: After that I will walk up to him and spit in his face—spit to my heart's content. Then, after that, I will give my woman some poison, and I will take some too and we'll both die. That's how it should be. When that happens, everything will be just right!

HENCHARĀLA: (*frowning*) This is a little complicated. You see, all the men who sleep with your wife are now your enemies. I will have to engage a big force if we are to catch them red-handed, so they can't give contradictory evidence. We will have to stay awake all night laying traps to catch them.

COMPLAINANT: I have money … no problem about the expense.

The junior clerk takes a big envelope from the desk and spreads it out.

HENCHARĀLA: According to this plan, show us where your woman hangs out most of the time.

While the complainant, the officer and the 2nd officer are studying the map, Manuvansa, shovel in hand, rushes on stage from the right front, shouting loudly.

MANUVANSA: A leg … a leg … there is a leg. Good god a new freshly cut-off leg … I saw it … I saw it … I saw it just now, good god!

FIRST SUBORDINATE OFFICER: What is this? Where are you running. Stop … stop

MANUVANSA: Hurry … Hurry … one must hurry.

FIRST SUBORDINATE OFFICER: Stop. Who are you?

MANUVANSA: I am Manuvansa.

HENCHARĀLA: (*angrily*) What are you doing man? What's all this bellowing? (*curiously*) What's that weapon you have in your hand?

MANUVANSA: It's a shovel for collecting garbage.

HENCHARĀLA: (*walking up to him*) Did you come in here thinking that we were garbage?

At that moment, Bunjā and Bahitē carrying the garbage bin and chasing after Manuvansa rush on stage. They cannot stop themselves and nearly bang into the officer. The security officer, the complainant, the Reverend, the first and second subordinates, and the rest of the crowd get quite upset, hold their noses and angrily shout at them.

What, are you mad to come here looking for garbage? Get out at once.

Instantly, Bunjā and Bahitē, terrified, run to a corner of the stage and look eagerly at what Manuvansa is going to do.

MANUVANSA: Sir, there is a leg, I saw it … I saw a leg.

HENCHARĀLA: (*indifferently*) Was that all you saw? Didn't you see the rest? Whose was it?

MANUVANSA: It was a man's leg, cut off from below the knee. I saw it …

HENCHARĀLA: Ah, a complaint, a complaint. Stand in the queue until the other complaints have been heard. Stand aside and wait.

Meanwhile, the security officer and the others study the map curiously and continue the discussion. Manuvansa walks up and down restlessly. Bunjā and Bahitē try to make signs to Manuvansa but he ignores them.

MANUVANSA: Please, sir. Hurry.

FIRST SUBORDINATE CLERK: Wait man. Don't cause trouble. Just wait a bit.

MANUVANSA: You haven't understood what I've been trying to say. This is what …

FIRST SUBORDINATE CLERK: Can't you do as you are told? Wait there quietly. I won't tell you a second time.

Manuvansa paces up and down impatiently. Meanwhile, a priest, Vahansē, has completed his work and as he is about to leave, Manuvansa goes to him.

MANUVANSA: Please Your Reverence, a terrible crime has been committed. There is a man's cut-off leg lying there—there—by the roadside. Does Your Reverence understand what I am saying? These officers do not seem to have understood. Can one just look on? Your Reverence understands what I am saying, don't you?

VAHANSĒ: My son, friend, brother, good man! May the blessings of the gods be with you! I will make a firm prayer that all the gods will give their blessings to bring about a solution to your problem.

MANUVANSA: No, no, no, no. Your Reverence also has not understood. This is not my problem.

VAHANSĒ: Then my friend, by the blessings of the gods there is no problem here.

MANUVANSA: No, no, Your Reverence, this is what has happened. There is a freshly cut leg, cut from the knee down, still dripping blood. It is lying at the edge of the road with the garbage … this is a most inhuman act. It is a man's leg after all.

VAHANSĒ: True, true. In god's name that is not a humane act.

MANUVANSA: (*somewhat relieved*) That's right. That's it. Your Reverence has understood. This … this is horribly ugly, shameful, disgusting. Behind this some enormous, horrible crime must have been committed. It might even be a conspiracy. If you hurry the murderer could be close by. You can get him. Hurry, hurry! Your Reverence, you come too. In the name of humanity make these others understand.

VAHANSĒ: You may be right. But neither religion nor the gods can interfere with the law. If you are the complainant, you will have to make the report. Talk it over with the Security Department and if there is a murderer find him. What I can do is organize a service in memory of the dead man. However, it may cost you some money.

MANUVANSA: No, no. I have no connection with the man killed or the killer.

VAHANSĒ: Then why are you worried about it?

MANUVANSA: No one seems to understand me. I did not come to solve my problem or to solve someone else's problem. I came to report a terrible ugly crime that has been committed.

VAHANSĒ: These days, there is a lot of work to be done in the place of worship. We are presently constructing a high wall around the premises, so I have to go now.

He is about to leave. Manuvansa pulls him by the hand.

MANUVANSA: No, no, please don't go. You must stay. In god's name, stay! You might think I am lying … don't go. Please wait. Take a look at the leg first.

VAHANSĒ: My son, I have far more important work to do than to look at a leg. Besides, I have seen more things than a leg.

MANUVANSA: Please sir, Hurry, Hurry!

FIRST SUBORDINATE OFFICER: You there, go away. Come back another day. We have finished taking statements for today. We have several other urgent things to do now.

MANUVANSA: Please try to understand. This is not my problem.

HENCHARĀLA: (*angrily*) If it is not your problem what you mother's son are you making such a fuss about? (*He comes forward and looks at Manuvansa closely.*) You seem a somewhat queer bird. (*indifferently*) Have you a name?

MANUVANSA: Yes, I'm called Manuvansa.[4]

All laugh.

HENCHARĀLA: Manuvansa. A strange name … Now Manuvansa, what is it we have to do? What is it you want us to do?

MANUVANSA: Sir, there is nothing I want for myself … but …

HENCHARĀLA: (*surprised and angry*) Man, if there is nothing you want personally and this is not your problem, take that stinking shovel and get out of here. Go to the ends of the earth. Vanish!

MANUVANSA: Please sir, I beg of you, I worship you. Don't be angry. Give me a chance to talk.

HENCHARĀLA: (*calmly*) Right. Say what you have to say; be brief.

MANUVANSA: (*rapidly*) There by the edge of the road near the wall, in the garbage, there is the leg of a man cut from the knee down.

A long silence. Everyone stares at Manuvansa as if to hear what more he is going to say.

HENCHARĀLA: *(breaking the silence)* So?

MANUVANSA: So, in god's name is it right to let it be there?

HENCHARĀLA: *(completely surprised)* Then where do you want it to be?

MANUVANSA: Why, by heaven, have you not understood yet? The leg should be on its owner's body.

HENCHARĀLA: Right, right. What you want us to do is to fix it back on the owner's body. How do you expect us to do that?

MANUVANSA: I don't want you to do that. This is so horrible. See, sir, what if a crocodile or a dog were to drag it away—you won't be able to carry out any kind of investigation. There must be some big terrible mystery behind this incident. We must hurry.

HENCHARĀLA: I cannot figure out to whom this is important. I can't even understand if this is a complaint or what. *(to Manuvansa)* I'll tell you what. You go back and stay by the leg. If a crocodile or a dog comes drive it off. We have some important petitions to hear. When we finish the investigations on those we will come by that way. You look after the leg.

The officer and the crowd prepare to leave on some other business.

MANUVANSA: *(angrily)* I don't think there is a more important complaint in the whole world than this. I'm sure of that. By heaven why don't these people understand what I am saying? If they did would they ignore it like this?

Manuvansa looks around impatiently, then moves to the center of the stage and shouts aloud.

There is a leg cut off from below the knee lying at the edge of the road. The security Department is not doing anything about it.

FIRST SUB OFFICER: Hey man.

HENCHARĀLA: Shut up, you mad man.

SECOND SUB OFFIER: Catch that fellow.

VAHANSĒ: A strange man!

HENCHARĀLA: *(catching Manuvansa by his neck)* Where did this jackal come from? He is a terrorist. Who did you think we were?

MANUVANSA: Forgive me, sir, for shouting like that.

HENCHARĀLA: For shouting! What the devil do you think you are doing shouting out in public like that?

MANUVANSA: Please forgive me, sir. Something came over me when I saw that leg. It is a horrible sight.

HENCHARĀLA: Stop it. Why, you big boar, did we refuse to hear you? We only asked you to wait awhile as we had more urgent work than your leg to attend to. How many more complainants were there in the queue before you?

MANUVANSA: But what has happened here is a murder. A terrible crime has been committed. So, we must hurry.

COMPLAINANT: Sir, what about my case? The more we delay the number of my enemies multiplies.

HENCHARĀLA: True. True.

MANUVANSA: If it happens again as happened before and I begin shouting—then it would be a disgrace for you people.

HENCHARĀLA: Yes, yes, yes. That's true too. (*to Manuvansa*) You have caused chaos here with that god forsaken leg. Hm … let's go then to attend to your job. Remember no more screeching like a bird of ill omen.

MANUVANSA: Let's run, sir …

FIRST SUB OFFICER: This devil is an impossible pain. Now he wants us to run!

MANUVANSA: Please lets run … quickly. (*To the priest*) You come, too, Your Reverence by God's grace. (*to Bunjā and Bahitē*) Come on. Come on you fellows.

Manuvansa urges everyone on, and leaves the stage. A staff officer removes the chair off stage. Bunjā and Bahitē take the bucket of garbage and exit from the rear. Manuvansa leading the group walks in front of the audience and leaves through the exit door of the auditorium.

Scene 3: The wall at the edge of the road

Instantly, the net walls are pulled away and two pieces of brick wall appear in their place. A dog, while he makes dancing gestures, at times barks at the leg and at others takes it in his mouth and dances, and yet again bites and eats parts of it. The dog is obviously delighted with his find. This scene plays for a short while.

Immediately thereafter the crowd rush in from the rear of the stage, see the dog and stunned can barely stop. Manuvansa heads the group. As they come on stage, the dog stops his dance, scowls and growls at them. The group cautiously eyes the dog and the leg. Manuvansa is even more upset and excited.

MANUVANSA: Good Lord! A dog is eating the leg. Get away you wretched beast.

He tries to hit the dog with his shovel. The dog fiercely drags the leg closer and snarls at Manuvansa.

HENCHARĀLA: Quiet, don't make a noise.

FIRST COMPLAINANT: (*indifferently*): There is only a leg there.

FIRST SUB OFFICER: This creature looks a very well fed animal.

SECOND SUB OFFICER: Cute dog!

BUNJĀ: (*to Bahitē*) Manuvansa is an idiot.

BAHITĒ: He is about to start a meaningless row.

Manuvansa again angered tries to hit the dog.

HENCHARĀLA: Stop it you fool. Stand back.

VAHANSĒ: It is a grave sin to commit acts of violence against this creature. One must show compassion and loving kindness towards all creatures.

MANUVANSA: That's what I say too.

HENCHARĀLA: Will you all be quiet and let me clear my head. You see the dog has already taken ownership of the leg.

MANUVANSA: What right has the dog to claim ownership of the leg? This is not a dog's leg. Get away you flea-ridden creature or I'll hit you!

The dog growls and again pulls the leg closer to him.

HENCHARĀLA: You keep back. We will sort this out quietly with the dog. This is not a flea-ridden dog. Think about it. This is no common or garden dog. Do you see the tag on his neck? It is a dog owned by someone who cares for it. So, we have to do our work cautiously.

Hencharāla whistles to the dog and talks to it gently. In response, the dog growls and barks at him.

MANUVANSA: Sir, it's no use talking gentlemanly language to this animal. We must kick him in the arse and drive him away. What is important for us is not the dog but the leg.

VAHANSĒ: I do not condone hurting the animal. That is a sin.

COMPLAINANT: What is important about this leg that has no owner? Whereas in my case, every second of delay, means that my enemies multiply. (*to Manuvansa*) Man, my family life is being destroyed because of your futile business that is eating up our time.

MANUVANSA: This is not my personal business man. (*to the officer*) Sir, record my statement even now and begin this investigation.

HENCHARĀLA: Yes, yes, let's do that.

FIRST SUB OFFICER: Let's do that. Let's do that.

SECOND SUB OFFICER: That's the way to go.

COMPLAINANT: Sir, Finish this damn thing quickly and let's go settle my affair.

HENCHARĀLA: Good. First, who saw this leg? Ah! I've forgotten to bring my record book. Has anyone got a piece of paper?

Everyone looks around. Bunjā hunts in the garbage and takes out a small piece of paper, which he hands over to the officer.

Oh good. This will do. (*He gets ready to write.*)

Oh dear, it's hard to write without my table.

To Manuvansa.

You there, bend over. Bend over a little.

Manuvansa bends over, places his hands on his knees and waits.

Yes, now make your statement.

MANUVANSA: First of all, this morning Bunjā, Bahitē and I were collecting the garbage and came to this place. I think it was about 8 o'clock.

BUNJĀ: Sir this was the first day that this fellow came on the job.

MANUVANSA: Sir, put that within brackets.

HENCHARĀLA: I will write it within brackets. You make your statement. Be brief.

MANUVANSA: So, when I came to this place I saw this leg lying there. Ah! Now that dog is eating that leg.

Manuvansa while talking is closely watching the dog and the leg.

HENCHARĀLA: Stop wriggling man. (*He gives Manuvansa a knock on his head.*) Then what happened?

While he is writing his pen now runs dry. He licks it to wet it, then scribbles on Manuvansa's head and back to check if it works, and proceeds to write.

MANUVANSA: Then when I saw that, I was overcome with a strange feeling. In all my life I have not trembled like that. Then I thought, Heavens, this is a terrible crime. The murderer should be hit by lightning. The son of a bitch who did this, how could he bring himself to do such a thing? Had he no humanity? After all this is a human life, a son of a mother and a father who nurtured him with love from childhood, now lying in the garbage? Where is the rest of this man's body, I thought?

HENCHARĀLA: Stop it, man. We are not interested in your thoughts.

MANUVANSA: But, sir, how can I keep such thoughts in my head?

HENCHARĀLA: Stop bothering us and tell us what you know.

MANUVANSA: Sir I don't know any more than what I saw there.

HENCHARĀLA: (*pushing Manuvansa away*) Then get out of the way without inventing stories. I can't think what kind of a fellow this is. There is nothing he seems to know. Just wastes people's time.

MANUVANSA: There, there, the dog is eating the leg again.

HENCHARĀLA: OK, OK. Don't get excited. I will get the leg for you.

MANUVANSA: Sir, I don't need that leg.

A sudden silence.

HENCHARĀLA: I have no use for it either.

MANUVANSA: What is the meaning of this, sir? (*turns to Vahansē*) Did you hear what he said? Where is his humanity?

VAHANSĒ: True, true. That does not seem a very humane thing to say.

Everybody agrees.

HENCHARĀLA: Yes, yes, it does not fit very well with one's humanity. (*Meanwhile, there is a sound from back stage. Engelsina enters.*) Smile … Smile … Smile … Smile … Where are you? Where are you my little one? … Smile ….

Everybody with great interest and curiosity turns towards the sound. Meanwhile, the dog barks loudly three times. Engelsina comes to where the people are, sees the dog biting the human leg and is aghast.

ENGELSINA: Oh my god, Smile! Why do you roam around these streets? Oh my, Smile! Why are you eating this horrible garbage? Why my little one, (*tearfully*) didn't I raise you on Australian bacon and New Zealand milk. My little baby whom I nursed on my lap, how could you have sunk to these depths? How can I kiss you when you eat such horrible muck? Did you eat the rest of this man too, Smile? No, no, no, my Smile does not eat such rotten stuff. Please rescue my Smile. Why do you all stand there staring like scarecrows? Aren't there men whose job it is to clear up such muck? I'm going to report to the Mayor that his workers are not doing their job. (*to the dog*) Oh my, Smile, how did you come to this pass?

MANUVANSA: Lady, if you would take your "*Mile*"[5] and leave now, it would help. Don't you see there is a criminal investigation taking place here? If he won't give us back that leg, I will beat him till the "*Mile*" falls off his back.

ENGELSINA: Who are you man, who's going to beat my dog till his fur falls off? (*to the security officers*) You are security people aren't you? Is this how you protect us? Do you know what this kind of dog is worth? I brought him when I returned from Sweden. It is the world's rarest breed.

Manuvansa tries again to drive the dog away with his shovel.

Don't you dare do that. He is not used to being beaten. (*turning to Manuvansa*) Who is this wild man? My poor Smile will now get an upset stomach. He only eats bacon, sausage and roast beef.

HENCHARĀLA: (*kindly*) Madam, don't worry. Nothing will happen to your dog.

The dog growls and again chews on the leg. Manuvansa again jumps to drive the dog away and the security officer pushes him aside. Manuvansa and the crowd become restive.

MANUVANSA: Sir, aren't you going to complete the rest of this murder investigation?

HENCHARĀLA: Ah yes, we were in the middle of a murder investigation. Let's go back to that. Tell me your name, madam.
(*to Manuvanasa*) Come here man. Give me your back.

Manuvansa comes, bends low again, braces his hands on his knees and waits. But his attention is fixed all the while on the dog and the leg. The rest of the group wait anxiously to see what happens next. The security officer writes.

ENGELSINA: Englesina.

HENCHARĀLA: And Smile's name is …

ENGELSINA: (*angrily*) Smile!

HENCHARĀLA: (*meekly*) Forgive me. Age?

ENGELSINA: I'm 62 years. Smile is five years.

HENCHARĀLA: When did you return from Sweden?

ENGELSINA: Four years ago.

HENCHARĀLA: Do you have children?

ENGELSINA: Yes, one. He is in London.

MANUVANSA: There, that dog is eating the leg again!

HENCHARĀLA: (*pulling at his head*) Stay still man, stop wriggling so I can continue with this investigation. (*to Engelsina*) Are you married?

ENGELSINA: (*angrily*) Do you think I had a child without being married?

HENCHARĀLA: Forgive me. Then what does your husband do?

ENGELSINA: He divorced me.

HENCHARĀLA: What a pity. What was the cause of the divorce? Was it a sexual matter?

ENGELSINA: What has that got to do with anything here man? (*She runs to the dog. The dog takes the leg in its mouth and runs off.*) Smile, come here, don't be headstrong.

MANUVANSA: (*He picks up his shovel and chases behind the dog.*) There the dog is running off with the leg. Stop it, you Mila!

ENGELSINA: Smile, drop that leg and run.

VAHANSĒ: Why is there no kindness, compassion or mercy in man? In God's name stop, Manuvansa. Don't hit the dog.

MANUVANSA: Drop that leg, you Mila. Drop it.

The dog seems to enjoy having the men shouting and chasing after him. The dog runs across the stage. Then as if to music he dances. Then he runs backwards. Manuvansa gives him a kick from the back and the dog falls off stage into the wings. The dog's shouts are heard and the crowd runs in that direction.

Scene 4

With the same lighting the scene changes to the security office. The two sub officers take two chairs and place it beside the table. Hencharāla is asleep with his head on the table.

Manuvansa enters. There is a plaster on his leg.

MANUVANSA: Sir … Sir …

HENCHARĀLA: (*sleepily*) Who is it?

MANUVANSA: It's me.

HENCHARĀLA: So …

MANUVANSA: I came several times to inquire what happened about the leg. I didn't get any information. Were there no results?

HENCHARĀLA: What results? Wait a little till I wake up.

There is a short silence. Manuvansa is impatient.

MANUVANSA: (*a little louder*) Sir.

HENCHARĀLA: (*Startled*) What is it man? (*wakes up*)

MANUVANSA: Sir … about that leg …

HENCHARĀLA: What leg? … Ah you have come again today. How many times have I told you that now there is nothing more for you to do about that matter? We will look into it.

MANUVANSA: How many times have I come here now? But still there are no results.

HENCHARĀLA: So, what good does a result do you? Do you at least get some money or profit from it? Not even that. Apart from the fact of having seen it you have no connection to the event. It is not your leg nor is it the leg of anyone you know.

MANUVANSA: Are you saying that if it is not my leg you will not make any more inquiries?

HENCHARĀLA: We are inquiring into it fellow, even though we don't keep telling you about it.

MANUVANSA: But all this time you have come up with nothing. Not even a hair's breadth of evidence.

HENCHARĀLA: It's not as easy as you think. (Somewhat firmly) All I want to know is this. How does this event affect you that you are so involved with it? Tell me that. Just tell me that.

MANUVANSA: I am a human being. I have a brain.

HENCHARĀLA: I also have a brain.

MANUVANSA: I have a heart.

HENCHARĀLA: I, too, have a heart.

MANUVANSA: From the day I saw that thing, something strange that I don't understand has happened to me. That was a human life. I cannot wipe it off my mind. At night in my dreams I see one or other of the murderers. I feel as if they are everywhere. I see mothers rocking their babies. In the middle of that I see that jackal of a dog playing with the leg. I see his mouth. I see the blood.

HENCHARĀLA: I also see such weird dreams now and then. Don't take them too much to heart. Keep a knife under your pillow and sleep.

MANUVANSA: (*somewhat angrily*) Even if I were to stick a knife under my clothes I would not come up with a solution to this mystery. After that day I could not continue to go to work for more than three more days. I've spent my time following up on this matter and now I have no money left either. How many times have I come to this office? I went to that temple and paid for 12 ritual ceremonies. That fraud of a priest, talking all the time about one's humanity and the blessings of the gods took all my money. Nothing came of it for me or for the gods.

At this point Vahansē comes rushing in from the front of the stage, very excited.

VAHANSĒ: (*seeing Manuvansa*) Ah, there he is. I saw him coming this way and thought I would catch him here. Write this down, sir, write this down. This madman has just come after flinging my golden god statue on the floor. O ye gods, the golden god statue is now completely broken at the neck.

HENCHARĀLA: What?

MANUVANSA: Liar, you rogue of a priest. You cheated me. He said I had to invoke the gods on this matter and tricked me and made me spend my money. He talked of the misfortune that had happened to the owner of the leg and made me perform rituals for him.

HENCHARĀLA: First tell me, which religion do you follow?

MANUVANSA: I don't know now what god to believe in. But whatever I do I cannot put my mind at rest.

VAHANSĒ: Sir, no one has ever before insulted the gods as he has just because he cannot put his mind at rest. I've tried to explain to him all the basic tenants of the doctrine of cause and effect that I know. I told him as best as I could about *karma*, the law of cause and effect. I taught him about the doctrine of *anātma* or "no soul."[6] But in spite of all that this fellow cannot accept what happened with the leg. In short, this fellow has no soul. I have performed all my obligations as a monk. With all that, this fellow suddenly rushes in this morning, picks up that golden statue and smashes it on the floor, saying that in addition to all the other weird dreams he is now seeing dreams of gods.[7]

HENCHARĀLA: I have performed all my duties as a security officer. Even though this man had no business to be involved, I conducted an investigation into this matter. As I see it now it is a question of his coming to terms with it mentally. As a security officer I have not learned to heal people's minds. It's none of my business. Besides, it is not my job.

VAHANSĒ: What this man must do now is go consult a doctor.

Manuvansa is staring hard at the monk.

MANUVANSA: Please don't get me angry. When I get angry I can't control myself. Now you all have aroused my anger several times. Neither gods nor doctors can put my mind at ease. Don't think I'm such a fool. I am a human being.

HENCHARĀLA: Why man we are also human beings.

MANUVANSA: Then didn't that leg, too, belong to a human being?

HENCHARĀLA: (*very angry now*) Are you suggesting that we are to blame for it?

MANUVANSA: I don't know which son of a bitch is to blame. But having seen that horrible leg I cannot put my mind at rest.

HENCHARĀLA: Good. So, if, as you say, we find out how this incident occurred, will that put your mind at rest?

MANUVANSA: Then I can sleep free of doubts and fears. Who will guarantee now that the world around me is a just and fair one? That I can expect to live a secure and stable life? In this present insecure unstable environment how can I live with a mind at peace? Until we find the murderer who committed this crime we have to suspect every man. How can I trust any man? How can I love another human being? (*to Hencharāla*) Do you understand that this is a question of love? Please solve this crime. Can you imagine what the owner of the leg suffered when it was cut off. Saw this too in a dream. The man screamed.

Manuvansa acts out what a man feels when he is tortured and his leg cut off.

This is how he yelled. 'O my god, O my precious mother, save me, save me. Stop, stop. O … that hurts so. It burns through me … If I have done any wrong punish me. Don't do this. Don't destroy my life which I can never get back again. O god I can't bear it …

Meanwhile, watching Manuvansa's performance Hencharāla laughs hysterically. Manuvansa stops.

Why do you laugh?

HENCHARĀLA: (*laughing*) Excellent. You performed that very realistically. A fine actor! Do it again. What a great piece of acting.

MANUVANSA: Good god! What kind of a man are you? Why don't you feel any of the fears and doubts I feel?

HENCHARĀLA: It is to quell our fears and doubts that we have weapons. I will give you a weapon for your protection. Keep it always close at hand.

He is about to open the table drawer to take out a weapon.

MANUVANSA: (*angrily*) How can a weapon put one's fears and doubts to rest? If I keep a weapon with me the other fellow will live in fear and have doubts about me.

HENCHARĀLA: (*also angry*) Then I will give the other fellow also a weapon.

MANUVANSA: Are you then planning to destroy the whole world?

HENCHARĀLA: I can say for sure that you are definitely sick. I don't know what the sickness is. I know of no man who does not walk free of fears and doubts when he carries a weapon. You should go quickly and consult a doctor.

MANUVANSA: All of you will have to answer for this. You are a worthless human being. The sick man is not me, it is you. Are you trying to save your skin by calling me a sick man? You better know that until I get results I will not easily let go of this matter.

HENCHARĀLA: (*very angry now*) You are a mad man. I have never in my whole life met such a pest as you. Why, you son of a bitch, you spend all this money, pursuing a matter that is no concern of yours. Didn't you know we even put an ad. in the papers saying, "Found a leg. Let the owner please report to the Security division."

MANUVANSA: What! An owner?

HENCHARĀLA: Yes. What use would it be for anyone else?

MANUVANSA: So where is that leg now?

HENCHARĀLA: (*looking around and also examining Manuvansa's legs*) I think it must be somewhere around. What's it to you? You have two legs. You can't walk with three.

MANUVANSA: You blockhead, idiot, bum, pig! Who gave you a certificate recommending you to this post? I'm quite sure you don't even have a birth certificate.

He leaves hastily.

HENCHARĀLA: (*furious shouts after Manuvansa as he leaves*) Know this you arsehole! No one has as many stars as I have. There aren't as many even in the sky! (*relaxed and to Vahansē*) I didn't do too badly did I?

VAHANSĒ: No not at all.

HENCHARĀLA: Poor fellow that. He is going to fall into big trouble. I tried as hard as I could to save him and send him away, but the fellow will not let go of this. If he comes to undermine our jobs we will let him have it. A strange difficult fellow!

VAHANSĒ: He has a heart of gold but the brain of a water buffalo.

Scene 5

The lights remain the same. As the two netted walls are removed two ornamented walls that suggest the home of a lawyer, appear on stage. Manuvansa and his lawyer are there. Around them are two small chairs. The lawyer smokes a pipe.

MANUVANSA: That is the story, sir.

LAWYER: Then is it against the chief security officer that you are going to bring this case?

MANUVANSA: As I see it is he not the person against whom we have to bring this case? He is the one at fault. He is a big dumb idiot. He says I'm a sick man and tries to avoid the issue. I think he has no understanding of how to investigate this matter. That dumb mule has still not been able to come up with even a hair's breadth of information regarding this crime. But the snake claims to have more stars on him than there are in heaven.

LAWYER: Don't you be afraid. We can win this case. It's a good thing that you came to me even if only by chance. Have you ever heard of a case that I have lost?

MANUVANSA: No.

LAWYER: What about cases I have won. Have you heard of any?

MANUVANSA: No.

LAWYER: In what far corner of the earth have you been living man?

MANUVANSA: I have come to this province only recently. Formerly, I lived in a small village in a distant region. From the time I can remember I lived with my mother in a children's home. My mother was the teacher in that home. I learned what I know from her. Though my mother taught me everything, because of her great love for me she did not allow me to associate with anyone outside the children's home. When mother knew she was about to die, she got me married to a woman from this region. In the province where I lived, if I ever saw a dead man he would be in a coffin. That, too, in a most civilized way, with his hands folded like this. Even in the case of a fellow who ran around naked all his life, when he was in his coffin he had all his clothes on and a flower pinned here.

LAWYER: Upon my mother! … However, don't imagine that this is an easy case. We have not a shred of evidence as to how that leg came to be there.

MANUVANSA: What then?

LAWYER: Then do you insist that we make this security guy the accused? (*in a low voice*) Shall we cook up some evidence and make some other fellow the accused?

MANUVANSA: (*amazed*) What are you saying, sir?

LAWYER: A chief security officer is a man who does the bidding of the government. If you make him the accused, you are bringing a case against the government. Neither you nor I can come up with evidence to prove the government wrong. The best way to go is to make some fellow not connected with this, the accused. That would make it much easier for me and better for your future.

MANUVANSA: That is a very strange thing to say. I don't need to take revenge on any man. Besides, by accusing a man who is unconnected with this crime what good does that do to him or me or the world? Just think a little, sir. If one gives a sharp knife to a monkey in order to protect men, what would happen?

LAWYER: The question now for me is this. Why is it that only you cannot make up your mind to forget the matter?

MANUVANSA: That is the question that is haunting me too, sir. But don't you feel that in the name of humanity we can surely win this case?

LAWYER: A thought has just struck me. Yes, we can win this case. We have done harder cases than this. We once proved that a murder was committed by a mortar and that the gun used was a pestle. These are hardly issues. The question is the cost. What kind of money do you have?

MANUVANSA: All we have is a very small house and a piece of land that goes with it, which does not even have a yard. I started a job but could not continue for more than two or three days because of this problem. We now live on what little money we got from pawning my woman's earrings. So, for any further work all I have left is my small house.

LAWYER: From what you say, the money you can get from selling the house will not be enough to pay for this case. I charge to win not to lose a case.

MANUVANSA: Sir, you say this is a very difficult case, but I don't think so. Even a child knows that finding a cut off leg beside the road indicates a crime has been committed. It is not right that one should do this to a human being.

LAWYER: (*in a deceptively conciliatory tone of voice*) True. This is an inhuman act. One should never permit such acts.

MANUVANSA: If I sell my house and plot of land I won't have anywhere to live. I will mortgage it.

LAWYER: Then how will you redeem it later?

MANUVANSA: After this case is over, and I go back to my job I will pay it off little by little. Please, sir, now that I don't have any money, can I mortgage it to you?

LAWYER: (*thinking it over for a while*) Good. It doesn't matter then. Since that was an inhuman act, let us do this in a humane way. After all, we must give priority to one's humanity. An act in the name of humanity is after all the noblest, highest, most worthwhile act.

MANUVANSA: Now, sir, you have understood. When I think of all that has happened in the short time I have been here I begin to believe that we live in a vast, empty, useless, cowardly environment. In short, putting that leg in a garbage heap indicates that our entire human race has reached a tragic pass. You understand that don't you? Do you think that one can look on such things and do nothing? A man's humanity is worth more than all the money, property, pearls and jewels, more than the whole world. Isn't that so sir?

LAWYER: Yes, for sure.

MANUVANSA: You understand then that when we no longer value our humanity there will be no world. Can one permit a dog to dance around with a human leg? One can't, can one?

LAWYER: That's for sure.

MANUVANSA: Therefore, as human beings we must protect our humanity. Isn't that so?

LAWYER: Yes, for sure.

MANUVANSA: Then when I try to talk to that security officer Hencharāla about man's humanity, is it right that he should call me sick or mad for pursuing a matter that does not concern me. Is it right that he should call me an arse-hole? Is it right he should abuse me like that?

LAWYER: Yes, for sure … I mean no, it is surely wrong that the man should abuse you like that. Whatever happens we must preserve our humanity.

MANUVANSA: Then, sir, I will now leave. I have to attend to several more things. So much so that I have hardly had time to sleep these days.

Manuvansa leaves. The stage becomes dark.

LAWYER: (*Shouts for joy as he walks into the house.*) Darling, darling, come here my precious. Our life is going to change now. I promise you, from now on we will not have to suffer living in rented houses. We can have a child. We will be happy. But promise me that you will not fight with me in future.

Interval

Scene 6

The courthouse. At the back of the stage where the judge should be seated there is a somewhat high wall. The back wall will be used for this. On the left front of the stage there will be a square upturned stool to act as the enclosure for the accused. A similar stool upturned will be on the right side of the stage as the enclosure for the prosecution. In the space between the enclosure for the accused and the judge's seat is a long low bench. A similar low bench will be placed between the prosecutor's enclosure and the judge. In the middle of the stage facing each other are two chairs for the two lawyers. The judge has not yet arrived. The witnesses for the accused (Hencharāla, his lawyer, the petitioner who complained about his wife, Engelsina, Vahansē, and the two subordinate officers) stand by the enclosure for the accused, chatting. Those for the prosecution (Manuvansa, his lawyer, and his wife) stand by the enclosure for the prosecution also chatting. The judge enters rapidly from back stage and takes his place. The judge suffers from a stammer.

JUDGE: S … s … s … silence. S … s … Silence.

The crowd stop talking and go to their allotted places. While Manuvansa's wife sits on the bench beside the prosecution enclosure, Hencharāla's supporters, all except his lawyer, sit on the bench beside the accused. Manuvansa climbs into the prosecution enclosure and Hencharāla climbs into the enclosure for the accused. While the case starts in this manner as it proceeds there are points where people walk all over the stage. All are silent.

JUDGE: The ch … ch … chief security officer of the p … p … province of Na … Na … Narugama, He … He … Hencharāla is the accused.

HENCHARĀLA: Yes, sir. That is correct.

JUDGE: The ca … ca … case for the p … p … p prosecution is brought by one Ma … Ma … Manuvansa, who is a … mu … mu … municipal cleaner for the city. He complains that he found a leg among the garbage and reported it to you but y … you took no action about the cr … cr … crime. Are you ga … ga … guilty or n … n … not guilty?

HENCHARĀLA: Not guilty.

MANUVANSA: (*amazed*) What?

MANUVANSA'S LAWYER: (*in a whisper*) That's how it is. Don't get excited.

JUDGE: Wh … wh … what do you have to say in defense?

HENCHARĀLA: Your Honor, this was not a crime.

MANUVANSA: (*even more amazed*) What the devil man!

LAWYER: (*In a whisper to Manuvansa*) That's how it is. Be patient. Don't make a row. You may be fined.

MANUVANSA: (*to lawyer*) If he goes on like this the fellow might even say there was no leg.

MANUVANSA'S LAWYER: Yes, that might be so. Be patient. But that is how it is with law cases. (*Manuvansa is becoming increasingly impatient. to Hencharāla*) So, if there was no crime did you find the man to whom the leg belonged?

HENCHARĀLA'S LAWYER: Your Honor, this is a strange and amazing petition. The prosecution has not brought any evidence to show how this leg came to be here. Besides, even though a notice was put in the papers saying that a leg was found and will the owner please come and claim it, no one has done so. Here, Your Honor, is the notice.

He pulls out a tattered piece of an old newspaper and shows it.

MANUVANSA: Your Honor I want to see that notice.

The piece of paper is given and Manuvansa stares at it reading it with difficulty.

Your Honor, this has been put in the short ads column. How can a man even see this small print? (*He counts the words.*) one, two, three ... eleven. There are only eleven words. Can a man's life be compressed into eleven words? Also, it states here "do not reply" within brackets!

HENCHARĀLA: Your Honor, sometimes when you put this kind of notice people respond just for fun.

MANUVANSA: When you put such idiotic notices, of course people will want to make fun of you.

HENCHARĀLA'S LAWYER: I like to remind Your Honor that this notice was paid for by the accused, not by the prosecution.

MANUVANSA: What you devil. Am I expected to do that too? (*to his lawyer*) Ask him, sir, how can he say this was not a crime. This was a most horrendous unspeakable crime.

The crowd becomes restive.

JUDGE: S ... S ... Silence. There is a lot of c ... c ... c ...confusion here. Let's try to s ... s ...sort this out. Is there a m ... m ... medical r ... r ... report on this?

HENCHARĀLA'S LAWYER: Yes, Your Honor. Here is a copy.

Hands a paper to the judge.

JUDGE: P ... p ... please read it.

HENCHARĀLA'S LAWYER: Shall I read it?

JUDGE: R ... r ... read it.

Hencharāla's lawyer opens a file takes out a paper and reads it aloud.

> This leg is a man's leg. It has been separated from the man's body at the knee. At the place where it was severed there are burn marks, bruise marks, marks of an explosive, scratch marks, marks of having been smashed by the tires of a vehicle, ant bite marks, dog bite marks, marks of a dog having pissed on it and several other marks that cannot be identified.

MANUVANSA: (*to himself*) Good god!

HENCHARĀLA'S LAWYER: (*continuing to read*) Yet, it is not clear whether any of those marks were made before or after the leg was severed from the body.

MANUVANSA'S LAWYER: Can he say what sex it is? That is if it is a man's leg or a woman's leg?

MANUVANSA: Yes, that's it.

HENCHARĀLA'S LAWYER: Your Honor, how can he tell that from this? Normally a person's sex organ is found not below the knee but above it. Any man here will confirm that.

JUDGE: Bu … bu … but a medical report must state the sex of the victim. Kindly r … r … read the rest.

HENCHARĀLA'S LAWYER: Shall I read it?

JUDGE: Yes yes yes.

HENCHARĀLA'S LAWYER: Yes, let's check again. It may be within brackets. (*He begins reading again.*) Forgive me, Your Honor, here it says. It is a male's right leg.

MANUVANSA'S LAWYER: What age?

MANUVANSA: That's right.

HENCHARĀLA'S LAWYER: It says the age is between 25 and 30 years.

MANUVANSA: I wish to see that report. (*It is given to him*).

He reads it and returns it.

MANUVANSA'S LAWYER: My question is this. How does the defense prove that this is not a crime?

MANUVANSA: That's right. Good.

HENCHARĀLA'S LAWYER: It becomes a crime only if this leg has been forcibly cut off from its owner's body. But from the medical report we cannot come to a firm conclusion as to how this leg was separated from the owner's body.

MANUVANSA'S LAWYER: But according to this medical report when the leg was brought for inspection it was already two days and one and a half hours old. We can thus tell that the leg was separated from the body on February 11th at about 1.30 a.m. You will agree on that point.

HENCHARĀLA: Yes.

MANUVANSA'S LAWYER: Accordingly, do you accept that it was the petitioner Manuvansa, who pressured you to send this leg for a medical report and that till then you did nothing.

MANUVANSA: That's it.

HENCHARĀLA: No, whether Manuvansa told me to do it or not I was going to do it.

MANUVANSA: That's a complete lie. If not for me there would not even be a leg ….

HENCHARĀLA'S LAWYER: Can you prove that?

There is complete silence. Everyone looks at Manuvansa. He remains silent.

HENCHARĀLA'S LAWYER: That means Your Honor that he cannot prove it.

MANUVANSA'S LAWYER: Your Honor. I ask that a clean report on the work done so far by this accused be presented to court.

MANUVANSA: Yes, that's right!

JUDGE: (*to Hencharāla*) To what extent and over how long a period can you clearly prove you have done your job efficiently.

MANUVANSA: Yes, yes, that's it!

JUDGE: I advise you strongly not to interject unnecessary comments.

HENCHARĀLA: Your Honor, I can produce three witnesses including the priest of the region who know the work I have done very well.

JUDGE: Kindly c … c … call them.

Vahansē, The First Subordinate Officer, the Second Subordinate Officer, and the former petitioner rise and stand beside Hencharāla.

Make a clear statement about the work of this security officer Hencharāla.

Before the judge can complete his order, all four proclaim together in unison.

ALL FOUR IN UNISON: This Hencharāla is the chief security officer of our area. Ever since we have known him, he has worked for the protection, peace, and cooperation, of us all, looked after our needs, given us food, drink, clothes, dwellings, more than what even mothers and fathers would do and without complaint, and we swear he performed his duties with kindness and full compassion. In addition …

JUDGE: Stop … s … stop … That's enough.

The witnesses go and sit on the bench.

HENCHARĀLA: They have stopped.

JUDGE: Send them out.

HENCHARĀLA: They have gone out.

MANUVANSA'S LAWYER: So, during this long time what information have you gathered about this leg?

HENCHARĀLA: There was not that much information. There was not a shred of evidence as to how the leg got there.

HENCHARĀLA'S LAWYER: Your Honor, there is no case here. When making inquiries it became obvious that this leg was not important to anyone.

JUDGE: Then how is there a p … petitioner?

HENCHARĀLA'S LAWYER: Your Honor, that is a curious question. I would like to know what connection there is between the petitioner and this leg.

Manuvansa looks at him, astounded.

MANUVANSA: What? Is that a question to ask?

HENCHARĀLA'S LAWYER: Yes, it is a question I'm asking.

JUDGE: You must answer the question. What is the connection between you and this leg?

MANUVANSA: (*amazed*) What is the connection?

HENCHARĀLA'S LAWYER: (*gleefully*) Your Honor, why does the petitioner from the day he found the leg, pursue this incident so doggedly even to the point of bringing a case?

MANUVANSA: I brought this case in the name of humanity.

All except Manuvansa's wife and lawyer, laugh aloud.

HENCHARĀLA'S LAWYER: He's brought a case in the name of humanity! (*laughs*)

JUDGE: (*to Manuvansa*) I warn you strongly, don't try to joke and make fun of this court. D … d …d … do you know the owner of this leg or someone connected to him?

MANUVANSA: No.

JUDGE: D … d … d … do you know how the leg came to be there or have you any clue or suspicion?

MANUVANSA: No.

HENCHARĀLA'S LAWYER: No … No … No. (*laughs*) Your Honor, you and everyone here have seen the facts. I firmly state that this is neither a crime nor a murder.

MANUVANSA: (*amazed*) What! Not a crime! (*to his lawyer*) Sir, now is the time to shoot with your pestle.

MANUVANSA'S LAWYER: Wait a little.

There is a solemn silence throughout the stage.

HENCHARĀLA'S LAWYER: Your Honor, how can this be a murder?

MANUVANSA: Are you saying that the owner of this leg is not dead? What crazy deaf and blind talk is this? You mean that man thought one of his two legs was extra, so he cut it off and threw it in the garbage! Your Honor, no man finds two legs too many. Even if he had three he would use that too to walk.

MANUVANSA'S LAWYER: That's true, Your Honor.

HENCHARĀLA'S LAWYER: Your Honor, there is no case here. Your excellency will agree that there are people in this world who can live without one arm. There are those who live without both arms. There are also those who live without both arms and a leg and there are those who live without both arms and both legs. Therefore, is it not possible for a man to live without a leg? The owner of this leg is very probably living happily in some place.

MANUVANSA: That cannot be. This is a crime, a murder.

JUDGE: (*to Manuvansa*) Q … Q …Quiet. Do not indulge in meaningless talk.

MANUVANSA'S LAWYER: Then how did this leg get separated from its owner?

HENCHARĀLA'S LAWYER: That I don't know. Besides, that is not our problem. Possibly it is the leg-owner's personal problem. Perhaps for some reason the leg was cut off and because a cut off leg was no longer any use it was thrown in the garbage and he is living with his other one leg.

MANUVANSA'S LAWYER: If that were so why does the medical report record cuts, scratches, burns, bruises? How did all that happen?

HENCHARĀLA'S LAWYER: After the leg was thrown out, it was possibly run over by some vehicle that night. It was probably burned by a cigarette stub someone threw away. When the dog was trying to eat it the cuts, scratches, bruises, breakages must have happened. How can this petitioner try to bring an inquiry about a leg that is of no interest even to its owner?

JUDGE: Has the P … P … P … prosecution anything to say to this?

MANUVANSA: That cannot be so.

JUDGE: Whether it is so or not is not legally valid. You must produce proof.

Manuvansa is about to say something when his lawyer forcibly shuts his mouth.

MANUVANDA'S LAWYER: Don't shout man. You will have to pay a fine too.

JUDGE: If that is so as the prosecution cannot produce any evidence, and as the defense has shown that the owner of the leg can have intentionally thrown it away, then this case is not a crime or a murder and so it is now di … di … di …

HENCHARĀLA: Dismissed.

JUDGE: That's right.

HENCHARĀLA: Your Honor, how can this case be simply dismissed? This man, latching on to a useless leg that is of no concern to anyone, has caused untold harassment and legal fees. I ask that you grant me compensation and costs.

Manuvansa seems to have reached a point of frenzied anger.

MANUVANSA: I'm to pay legal costs and damages! Me! I will not pay. Do what you want.

HENCHARĀLA: Yes, you must pay.

The crowd becomes restive and shout.

JUDGE: S … S … S … Silence.

The crowd becomes silent.

MANUVANSA'S LAWYER: Your Honor, this man brought this case in the interests of humanity.

HENCHARĀLA'S LAWYER: What crazy talk is that? This man, Manuvansa, on the basis of this useless leg, has humiliated and tarnished the image of this Security officer and his high office. That is clear from the dismissal of the case. Besides, this weird man Manuvansa hurled a golden image of the god, belonging to this priest, worth 750 lakhs, 7,500 hundred, smashed it on the floor and broke its neck. He has also abused this noble priest and humiliated him. Is that a humane act? Is that in the name of humanity?

MANUVANSA'S LAWYER: The petitioner has not done that. Can he prove it?

HENCHARĀLA: Is there proof?

JUDGE: (*to Manuvansa*) Are you innocent or guilty of this above-mentioned charge?

MANUVANSA: That I do not know. But it is true that I took that useless god's image and flung it on the floor.

HENCHARĀLA'S LAWYER: (*delighted*) He says he flung it on the floor. So, what more proof do we need?

MANUVANSA'S LAWYER: (*to Manuvansa*) You are a dumb idiot.

HENCHARĀLA'S LAWYER: Your Honor, that is not all. Because of his concern for this useless leg, this very strange man kicked the dog of a very rare breed, belonging to this cultivated lady named Engelsina and hurt its back. Is that a humane act?

JUDGE: Is there evidence? Can you prove it?

LAWYER: There is evidence. We can prove it.

JUDGE: (*to Manuvansa*) Are you guilty or innocent to this charge?

MANUVANSA: It was the first time in my life that I kicked anything—let alone a dog.

HENCHARĀLA'S LAWYER: You kicked it! Do you admit that it is wrong to kick and hurt animals?

MANUVANSA: Yes.

MANUVANSA'S LAWYER: You idiot.

HENCHARĀLA'S LAWYER: Your Honor, then there is no need of evidence on that count either.

The crowd shouts.

HENCHARĀLA: Your Honor, please award me my legal costs.

VAHANSĒ: Your Honor please obtain compensation for the damage done to the god.

ENGELSINA: Please award damages for Smile.

SUNVUNĀ/MANUVANSA'S WIFE: Please, Your Honor, have pity on Manuvansa.

MANUVANSA'S LAWYER: Manuvansa is innocent. Manuvansa is innocent.

JUDGE: S … s … s … silence. (*The crowd is quiet. to Manuvansa*) Are you p … p …p …prepared to pay c … c … c … costs and compensation for the damage you have done?

MANUVANSA: (*amazed*) Are you asking me?

JUDGE: (*angrily*) It's y … y …y … you I'm talking to.

MANUVANSA: They are asking me for more? I do not have even a gecko's egg left.[8] And if I had I would not give it.

JUDGE: In that case you will have to go to jail.

MANUVANSA: I cannot go to jail. That is unjust.

JUDGE: No that is the law. It is just.

MANUVANSA'S LAWYER: Your Honor, those acts were committed by this petitioner because of his simple mindedness. So he should not be put in jail.

HENCHARĀLA'S LAWYER: Forgive me Your Honor, but the dog that was beaten by this strange man is no ordinary dog. He is a rare breed. I ask that you conduct an investigation into that dog and award adequate compensation.

MANUVANSA: (*shouting*) It's no use talking of compensation. I have no money.

MANUVANSA'S LAWYER: Your Honor. The petitioner has no money.

HENCHARĀLA'S LAWYER: Then, Your Honor, should you not raise or lower his punishment in keeping with the value of the dog?

JUDGE: Is the d … dog owner here?

HENCHARĀLA'S LAWYER: Yes

JUDGE: Ca …ca … ca …

HENCHARĀLA'S LAWYER: Shall I call her?

JUDGE: Yes im … im … immediately.

Englesina walks and in stands in court.

JUDGE: Wh …wh … what have you to s … s … say about this matter?

ENGELSINA: He was all I had.

JUDGE: Wh … wh …who is "he"?

ENGELSINA: Smile.

JUDGE: Sm … Sm … Sm (*he sneezes*)

HENCHARĀLA'S LAWYER: Smile is the name of that dog.

ENGELSINA: Oh, I cannot speak. Everybody abandoned me. In the end it was only Smile who loved me. This miserable man kicked Smile.

She sobs. The stage is silent. Only her loud sobs are heard.

HENCHARĀLA'S LAWYER: (*softly to the judge*) Your Honor, the dog is now in the care of the veterinarian Dr Brumpy. He is here.

JUDGE: (*angry*) Ca ca … ca …

HENCHARĀLA'S LAWYER: Shall I call him?

JUDGE: Yes, yes, yes. (*to Engelsina*) Kindly go home and do your crying.

Engelsina bows her head and leaves. The veterinarian enters.

JUDGE: How long have you w … w …worked as a vet?

VETERENARIAN: I lived with animals from the day I was born.

JUDGE: De de … de … describe this breed of dog.

VET: (*Spreads a bundle of files on the floor. He takes up one at a time and describes.*) The scientific name for this breed of dog is Garshi Gothamanipa Vishtopi. This is a rare breed that is dying out in the world. To my knowledge, there is only one dog other than Smile, of this breed in this country. That is the chief minister's bitch, named Rosie.

JUDGE: How much is the dog worth?

VET: It is hard to give a monetary amount as they are so rare. I was hoping to start a new breed in this country with Smile and the chief minister's bitch, Rosie. That would be a matter of pride for our nation. Even the zoo does not have a specimen of this breed.

JUDGE: Stop. Briefly tell us the present condition of the dog Smile.

VET: Your Honor, the kick landed on the left side in the region between the rear thigh and the penis. The investigations in the intensive care unit revealed that 24 nerves were completely damaged. As a result, flow of blood to the kidneys and the bladder has been diminished. The bruise caused by the kick has penetrated from the outer skin to a depth of 6 centimeters, 9 millimeters, and 31 points internally. The dog is now in the intensive care section of the veterinary hospital. I have a full report of the condition of the dog in this file.

JUDGE: G … g … g … good. You can leave.

HENCHARĀLA'S LAWYER: When you consider the value of the dog shouldn't this man's punishment be increased? Your Honor, what an inhuman fellow this must be to have given the dog such a powerful kick?

MANUVANSA: When I kicked the dog, I did not have time to ask around about his value. The leg was already in the dog's mouth.

SUNVUNĀ: Your Honor, Manuvansa has a very soft, innocent heart. I know it well.

HENCHARĀLA'S LAWYER: This court is no place for your love talk.

SUNVUNĀ: What I say is the absolute truth. All this happened because of his humanity. Your Honor, whatever wrong he may have done was because he was so powerfully affected by the sight of the cut-off leg and had no way to express his dismay an distraught state of mind.

HENCHARĀLA'S LAWYER: Are we to blame for that? If his mind was distraught what he does to get over it is no concern of ours.

MANUVANSA'S LAWYER: Your Honor, you cannot put this man in jail. He is a human rights supporter.

HENCHARĀLA'S LAWYER: Your Honor, a man who can kick a most valuable dog until his back is almost broken, and can smash a golden image of a god worth 75 lakhs, 7,500 so that its neck breaks, what can such a man not do? This man, taking on an issue totally unconnected to him, bringing a court case against a most valued officer, smashing the image of a god whom millions worship, abusing a most noble and respected priest, breaking all rules and regulations, spending his last penny to bring a case single handed, against the government, how can this traitor, this cancer in the society be a human rights supporter?

The lawyers argue heatedly.

MANUVANSA'S LAWYER: Your Honor, can you not see that the petitioner's compassionate heart was so moved and mentally distraught at what he saw that the wrongs committed were the result of his distraught state of mind?

HENCHARĀLA'S LAWYER: In that case how dangerous it is to have such mentally distraught individuals in the society.

MANUVANSA'S LAWYER: It was his great feeling of humanity that made him act like this.

HENCHARĀLA'S LAWYER: How is it then that amongst this large population only he was moved in this manner?

MANUVANSA'S LAWYER: All this happened because of his deep humanity.

HENCHARĀLA'S LAWYER: Is this devil the only humane person in this world? Are the others not human?

MANUVANSA'S LAWYER: It is the petitioner's humanity, his humanity that is the issue.

HENCHARĀLA'S LAWYER: His inhumanity … The defense is innocent.

MANUVANSA'S LAWYER: You call that humanity!

The lawyers argue fiercely and hold each other by the throat.

JUDGE: S … s … s … Stop. S … s … Silence. (*Everybody is silent.*) T … t … taking the facts presented here into consideration, it has been proved that the man Manuvansa is legally guilty. S … s … Since he cannot pay the costs and damages he can be sentenced to eight years in prison with hard labor.

MANUVANSA: Your Honor, is there no way at all in this case for that man (*pointing to Hencharāla*) to be sent to prison and for me to be freed?

JUDGE: Only if you can prove that you were truly mentally distraught can you be released and that man be imprisoned.

MANUVANSA: (*to himself*) Good god! Can't a man be mentally distraught without having to find evidence to prove it?

SUNVUNĀ: Please Your Honor, don't send Manuvansa to prison. How will I live without him? From the very beginning I tried to explain to him the seriousness of these actions. In short I said "Don't go to court about other people's legs." But he would not listen. He has no idea how to live in these parts. Forgive him for this first offence. This comes of his foolishness, trying to protect a sense of humanity.

HENCHARĀLA'S LAWYER: That is just love talk. His actions were not that of a poor man.

MANUVANSA'S LAWYER: No, no, the petitioner is innocent. He is innocent.

At that moment, the crowd now with Engelsina, Vahansē, Hencharāla shout demanding compensation.

We want compensation. We demand compensation.

JUDGE: S … s … s … silence … silence.

MANUVANSA'S LAWYER: If there is a feeling of fear, suspicion and unrest among the crowd, Hencharāla is definitely responsible. Similarly, he should investigate the owner of the leg and he should know to bring him to justice.

HENCHARĀLA'S LAWYER: What nonsense is this. This leg is of no importance to the people. There is neither fear, suspicion nor concern among them. Manuvansa is a complete liar. He is involved in a personal feud with Hencharāla. He kicked the dog and smashed the god's image because of his barbaric inhuman personality. Or he did it as a scheme to use the situation of the leg to prove his great humanity.

MANUVANSA'S LAWYER: Then how can we know if he was mentally distraught or whether this matter is of importance to the people or not.

HENCHARĀLA'S LAWYER: The leg was lying by the edge of the road till 9:30 in the morning. Many other people would have seen it. But it was only Manuvansa who came to report it and even went so far as to bring a court case about it. Is it possible that in the whole country only Manuvansa was concerned about this? In that case the only man in the entire country who is humane is Manuvansa. That is a joke. How is it that it is of concern only to Manuvansa?

JUDGE: Th … th … that is the question here. M … M … M … Manuvansa, were you truly mentally distraught? Well, in what way were you distraught?
MANUVANSA'S LAWYER: Like this.

He acts as one who is terrified, then falls on the ground in a faint. The crowd look on attentively.

JUDGE: (*to Manuvansa*) Was it like that?
MANUVANSA: (*looks at the performance with curiosity*) No.

The crowd laughs.

MANUVANSA'S LAWYER: (*angrily*) I can't win this case with a fellow like you.

He walks out.

SUNVUNĀ: Please sir, don't go. This man can't understand. Don't go, please don't go.

She holds on to the lawyer's hand. The lawyer succumbs to pressure and sits down.

HENCHARĀLA'S LAWYER: (*to Manuvansa*) What happened to you when you saw the leg?
MANUVANSA: My hair stood on end. Some other strange things happened. However, I didn't write them down at the time.
JUDGE: H … h … how did your hair stand on end?
MANUVANSA: I didn't have time to examine it. Your Honor, if the law cannot come to a decision on me, put this case to the people who are gathered here. They will support me. If not, I will accept I was wrong.

The crowd moves towards the judge shouting.

JUDGE: S … s … s … silence … silence.
HENCHARĀLA: Your Honor, I, too, agree with that suggestion. Manuvansa, in the name of all humanity I challenge this performance of yours about your humanity. If you can, prove it and show it to us.
JUDGE: G … g … g … good. The two parties, the accused and the petitioner have agreed to put the decision to the people gathered here who have heard the case so far. Since they have listened so carefully I hereby appoint the people gathered as the jury on this case. What we want to know is this. Was Manuvansa truly mentally distraught or not? How was it that amidst such a large population he alone felt so emotionally distraught at the sight of the leg? Were you also moved to fear, suspicion and made mentally distraught by this sight? Or is Manuvansa a liar? M … M … Make a decision on the basis of the f … f … f … facts presented so far.

The lights in the auditorium slowly come on.

If there are five people who agree with Manuvansa, will they come up on to the stage? The jury can give their decision either by remaining silent or by coming on stage. We will have to accept your silence as your decision.

MANUVANSA: (*with great emotion addresses the audience*) Ye gods in heaven do you not have eyes and ears. Can five of you not come up on stage?

HENCHARĀLA: Your Honor, it does not matter if even three people are willing to come on stage.

HENCHARĀLA'S LAWYER: Are you mad, man! If even three people come up in support of Manuvansa we are done for.

HENCHARĀLA: (*smiling confidently*) Don't be afraid. That won't happen.

JUDGE: G … g … good. The defense has challenged three people to come on stage for Manuvansa. It is getting late. We cannot wait too long.

Silence in the auditorium.

HENCHARĀLA: Manuvansa, if you like you can go down close to the audience, talk to them and bring three people up on stage.

JUDGE: Yes Manuvansa, you have permission to go down to them.

A powerful silence fills the auditorium. Manuvansa looks at the crowd with great hopes, then slowly steps down and goes into their midst.

MANUVANSA: (*addressing the audience*) Amidst such a big audience why can't even three people come upon stage. Quick, hurry! (*silence*) Please, can't three people come in support of me.

Manauvansa almost in tears, walks down the middle and to the end of the center aisle and looks intensely at each person. Then speaking rapidly as if on the point of breaking down says

How can you all sit there and just look on?

Silence.

What is this silence that you are all jointly keeping? How much longer are you planning to sit there in silence? Or are you thinking that as in a play you can sit aside and just watch?

Silence pervades.

JUDGE: Time is passing. Please remember that we must register your silence as our reply.

MANUVANSA: Please, Your Honor, give me another moment. I am sure that there are at least three people here who are willing to stand up.

A powerful silence reigns.

HENCHARĀLA: (*raising a finger to Manuvansa*) Manuvansa, if you can get just one.

Silence persists. Manuvansa is breathing hard. Almost unconsciously, he comes towards the middle of the stage and stands below it. He does so having looked hard and expectantly at each one in the audience. Realizing that no one is going to come he rushes to the stage, bangs his head and arms on the stage and shouts. A powerful silence persists.

JUDGE: M … M … Manuvansa, will you now kindly come back on stage.

Manuvansa, overcome by feelings of despair, anger, sadness, walks a few steps up to the stage, looks hard at the audience and says in a low voice.

Somebody has silenced all of you and done it very well. They have carefully removed your backbone.

He rushes up to the stage, falls at the feet of the judge and weeping says:

MANUVANSA: Oh, my good excellent Lord, please free me, I beg of you. I worship you and promise that I will not do something like this ever again. Never, never again. I beg you let me go. Just let me go.

It is at this point that someone from the audience may stand up and move towards the stage. If this happens the alternate ending is performed. If not, the rest of this scene is enacted followed by scene 7.[9]

JUDGE: The a … a … a … accused is free. The p … p … p … petitioner is sentenced to eight years with one year's hard labor. Take charge of the prisoner.

The judge leaves abruptly. Two court officials come on stage, take Manuvansa by his arms and lead him out. Manuvansa turns for a moment and stares angrily at the audience as he is led away.

Scene 7

Inside Manuvansa's home. The upturned benches of the courtroom are now turned the other way to become benches. The other props are quickly removed. There are only two short bench-like seats made from narrow planks. Manuvana has his head and one arm bandaged. That hand is tied with a rope hanging from his neck like a sling. Manuvansa is seated on the bench upset and restless.

SUNVUNĀ: *(rapidly)* To whom can I tell all this. How are we now ever going to save our house and land? By trying to do the humane thing you ended up in jail for one and a half years. And till you came out I suffered all that one can humanly suffer, did every kind of work one can do to pay the mortgage and save the house.

MANUVANSA: *(in a fierce rage)* Stop that tin voice of yours, bitch.

SUNVUNĀ: A letter came from your workplace stating that you are a traitor, a rabble rouser, a madman and so you were being dismissed from your job. They say you are not right in the head.

MANUVANSA: Shut up, you she devil. When everything that could happen to a man has happened is it right that you should attack him like this, you rotten bitch.

SUNVUNĀ: That is why I kept telling you man from the very beginning, not to do such idiotic things. You dumb idiot. (*She is about to cry.*) Now we are finished, destroyed.

MANUVANSA: (*Kicks the bench he is sitting on and it turns over. He picks up with one hand a piece of wood that breaks off from the bench and tries to hit Sunvunā.*) Are you also coming to devour me? Know that I can kill you, cut you up and eat you.

SUNVUNĀ: Yes, eat me. There is now nothing to eat let alone anything left to get from me. (*She is about to cry.*) How much I tried to protect you. You must answer for this terrible disaster that has come on us.

MANUVANSA: I must answer? I? Know that I can kill you in one stroke.

SUNVUNĀ: (*shouts terrified.*) Good god, don't Manuvansa, don't!

MANUVANSA: (*grinding his teeth*) After all that has happened there is no space here, we cannot both live in this same house. It's either you or me. I will survive even if it means I have to kill you.

SUNVUNĀ: Remember, Manuvansa, there is nothing left now even for us to kill each other for.

MANUVANSA: Get out, you she devil. (*He flings the piece of wood at her. She runs out. After she leaves Manuvansa falls back on the bench and sits panting, disconsolate. A few moments later Bunjā, Bahitē and a doctor enter. The doctor is fully drunk. He can barely stand.*)

BUNJĀ: (*to Bahitē*) The man is in there.

BAHITĒ: Sir, doctor, here is the man, our friend, that we told you about. In the past he has had a lot of problems by trying to take on unnecessary things. (*coming up to Manuvansa*) There, your job question is settled. The mayor said that if you bring a medical report to say that your brain is sound, you can have your job back. So, we have brought a doctor. We can get him to write, not just your brain is sound but any other part you want certified, is also fine. He is a doctor from the government hospital. (*Manuvansa remains silent. To the doctor*) Then sir, let us begin to write.

BUNJĀ: (*He puts some money in the doctor's fist.*) Sir, keep this. It's just nothing.

DOCTOR: (*Taking it quickly and putting it in his pocket.*) Are you mad, Mister? We don't want money. We want men's … what was it I came here for? Ah yes, because of my humanity … Why did I drink today … because I was afraid I would have to do some inhumane act.

BUNJĀ: Please sit down here. (*He tries to seat the doctor on the bench but the doctor falls over, too drunk. He tries several times. Then he places the other bench beside the doctor, puts the pieces of paper he has brought on it, takes the pen out of the doctor's pocket and puts it in his hand.*) Now write.

DOCTOR: What should I write?

BUNJĀ: We want you to say that this man Manuvansa's mind is fine, and he is not mad. That he is as good as anyone.

DOCTOR: That won't be difficult. Let's see what we can do.

BAHITĒ: (*Aside to Bunjā.*) Bunjā you gave the doctor too much to drink. The devil can barely hold a pen.

BUNJĀ: Yes, it struck me too at the time. But this polecat kept drinking like a blind elephant in must![10]

DOCTOR: Let's write. Let's write. About what should I write? Is it about an animal or a man?

BAHITĒ: Doctor, we just told you. It's about a man.

BUNJĀ: Write the date here.

DOCTOR: It's this year is it? Here, Mister, hold on to this bench. It seems to have come alive. It is shaking. (*Bahitē holds it down firmly.*) What is the man's name?

BAHITĒ: Manuvansa of the house of Purity.

DOCTOR: Doesn't he have a shorter name? How can I write this kind of long name at a time like this? (*The doctor tries to write something and again falls over. Bahitē and Bunjā prop him up again.*) Now what do I write? You two will help me to write this, won't you? I don't have a thought in my head.

BUNJĀ: Write Manuvansa is an ordinary man.

DOCTOR: I can't spell "ordinary." Don't use big words. All you want is to certify that this man is a man.

BAHITĒ: That's it. If you write that Manuvansa is a man—that is more than enough.

DOCTOR: Hold on to this then. Fine. Now let's write. (*He tries to write and falls over again. They seat him upright again.*) It's not as easy as you think to obtain human status.

Alternate Ending[11]

(Alternate ending: Translator's note)

MANUVANSA: (*Addresses the audience from the auditorium. He shouts.*) Your Honor. There are people for me who feel my pain.

(*To members of the audience*) Come, come up on stage.

He leads them onto the stage and jubilantly with great excitement rushes triumphantly towards the judge.

Your Honor, look, look here …

At that instant, a deafening sound is heard as several shots are fired. Manuvansa falls. The court is in an uproar. People are shouting. The gunman is seen disappearing from a corner at the back of the auditorium. The crowd point in his direction and shout.[12] *Suddenly, all are silent. Everyone on stage slowly walks towards where Manuvansa lies dead. They stand in a half circle around him. They look a moment at him, then raise their heads, stare at the audience, and remain still. Slowly the stage darkens.*

Alternate Ending[13]

A wall beside a road. As in Scene 1, at the beginning of the play, Manuvansa appears together with two others, Ālē and Bālē, collecting garbage. It is clear that Manuvansa is now quite expert at the job.

MANUVANSA: Hey, look how beautiful these roads are. Nothing like what they used to be. Can't think what it was like then.

BĀLĒ: Shows how much the country has progressed.

ĀLĒ: Making the pavements was a great thing. It is as if we are now in England. Don't you feel a sense of pride for little Sri Lanka and how far we have come?

BĀLĒ: Of course I feel it.

ĀLĒ: Just recently, a Sinhala gent living in Australia and visiting for the holidays said that Sri Lanka was now as developed as Australia. Yes, and if not for the fact that they are no longer used to this climate, they would even think of coming back to live here. Doesn't that make you feel proud!

BĀLĒ: Of course it does.

ĀLĒ: By god! What a difference the roads have made.

BĀLĒ: What are you saying! Now when you pull your vehicle on to that highway to Matara, …

At this point Manuvansa has turned up a decapitated human head in his shovel.

MANUVANSA: It goes Whoosh … sh … sh … (*he says as he flings the head into the garbage bin. The others laugh loud.*)

The end

****

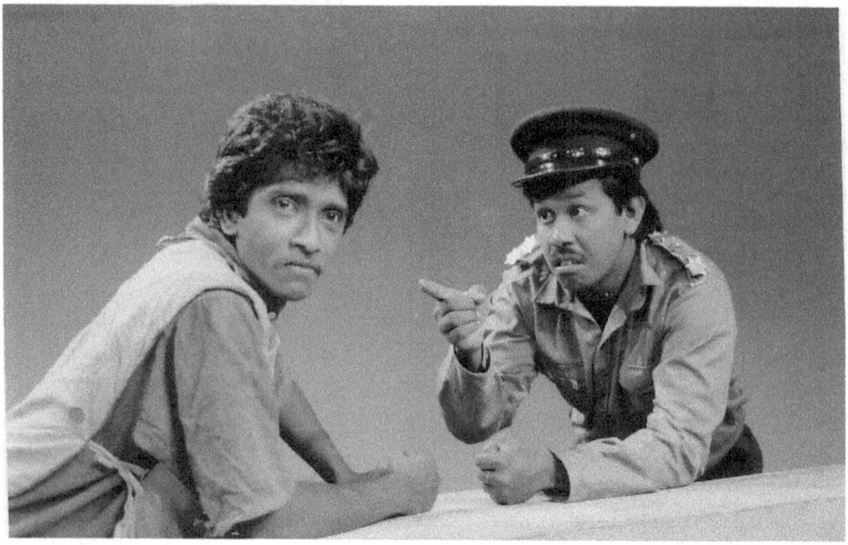

PHOTOGRAPH 3.1 Manuvansa and Hencharala in *The Juryy*. Photograph by Udeni Alwis

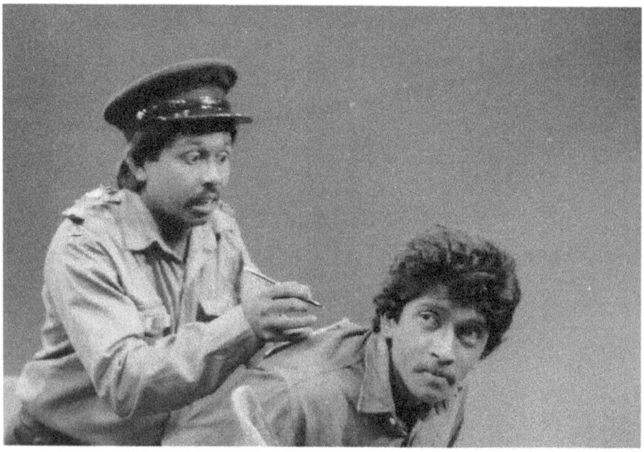

PHOTOGRAPH 3.2 Manuvansa and Hencharala in *The Jury*. Photograph by Udeni Alwis

Notes

1 One of the cheapest tobacco products available in Sri Lanka.
2 A passing critical comment on development and its implications.
3 In Sri Lanka, the water buffalo is considered the dumbest of oxen. He eats and sleeps in muddy water all day and the only work he does is walk round and round in a circle to plough or harvest rice fields.
4 Literally means "*manu*—human, *vansa*—clan": one who belongs to the human clan.
5 A play on the word "mile," which can refer to fur or body hair.

6 Buddhists do not believe in a "soul" or *ātman* distinct and separate from the physical body that takes on a life after death.
7 The Buddha did not claim to be a god, only a teacher. But he is popularly worshipped as a being with divine powers and often treated as a god.
8 A gecko's egg is very small. The idiom is intended to convey a very miniscule amount.
9 Translator's note:
Sri Lankan audiences at the time were not used to participating in the ongoing action of a play—as with Living Theatre performances in NY in the 70s or Boal's Argentinian performances. The fourth wall proscenium stage was what audiences were familiar with. Moreover, this play was first performed during what came to be known as the the *bhishana kalaya* or "time of terror" when there was a pervading atmosphere of fear in the country. The brutality of the para-military violence the government had unleashed against all forms of opposition, had silenced dissent. Thus though the play was intended as a political and social critique of the prevailing situation, the playwright did not expect any member of the audience to come on stage. The play was to conclude with scene 7. However, in one of the very early performances, a young man in the audience (I was told this by the director) suddenly decided to walk up to the stage in support of Manuvansa. Both the director and the actors were momentarily stunned and did not know how to proceed. It was at this point that the director brought the play to a brilliant close with the gunshot. Later, this was worked into the play and became an authoritative "alternate ending," to be used when one or more audience members walked onto the stage.
10 Young male elephants become crazy and uncontrollable when in heat.
11 On many occasions during performances of this play, at the end of this scene members of the audience do come up on stage in support of Manuvansa. Then the alternative ending is performed. This will depend on the situation. If one or more members of the audience walk onto the stage this alternate ending is enacted.
12 While some of this is staged, some of it a spontaneous reaction from the audience members. The amount of audience participation and actor-audience interaction depends on specific performances of the play.
13 This is a new ending sent by the dramatist in 2019.

★★★

Dhananjaya Karunarathne is a playwright, director and designer working as an independent artist in Sri Lanka and Australia. Dhananjaya brought his theater to Australia in 2004. He completed a Master of Creative Arts and a Master of Creative Arts Research degree in Theater at the University of Wollongong, Australia. Some of Dhananjaya's plays include *Last bus eke Kathawa/The Story of the Last Bus* (1999), *Sihina Rangahala/ Theatre of Dreams* (2008) *The Zoo Story Experiment* (2003). One of his most notable Australian productions is *A Sri Lankan Tamil Asylum Seekers Story as Performed by Australian Actors under the Guidance of a Sinhalese Director*, presented by Merrigong Theatre Company. Dhananjaya also has a great passion for teaching theater. He has refined his teaching style whilst conducting drama workshops across Sri Lanka as a workshop instructor and a visiting Lecturer in Theatre in universities in Sri Lanka. These teaching experiments have encouraged him to explore the actor-spectator relationship further. Currently, Dhananjaya is the founder, workshop instructor and artistic director of a Sydney-based theater movement called the Sydney-Colombo Theatre Project which is focused on developing theatre activities in the minority communities.

SHADOWS AND MEN (SEVANÄLI SAHA MINISSU 1993)

Prasanna Jayakody

Characters

DUNGURA: The Man
CHUKKINA: The Woman
DUNGU: The Man's mind
CHUKKI: The Woman's mind

Scene 1

The curtain is kept open before the play starts. On an upper level on the stage is a small room. On the left is a window that looks out on a populous city. On the right is a ladder by which to enter the upper room. The only piece of furniture on stage is a large chest or "pettagama." A tall stick is stuck on it and a lantern hangs on the end of the stick. A man sits on the chest with his back to the audience. He holds his head in his hands and is falling asleep. Meanwhile, a long rope strung from his shoulders runs through the middle of the auditorium to the very back.

As the first bell rings to start the performance a short piece of music is played followed by this mixed-Pali stanza:

Tamēca mātā pitātanca tamēca (You are my mother, my father)
Tamēca bandusca satātamca (My kinsmen and close friends)
Tamēca vidyā dravidam tamēca (My science and knowledge)
Tamēca sarvam ma deva deva (You are everything to me)

The stanza ends. The time is midnight. A clock strikes loud. The motionless man awakes. Slowly he raises a hand and increases the flame in the lantern. The ticking of the clock resembles the ticking of the man's heart. The man is looking for something. He is searching for himself. He is searching for his mind.

THE MAN (DUNGURA): Where are you? Dungu … Dungu … Dungu. It is your body Dungura that is talking to you. Can't you hear? I have looked for you throughout my entire body, but you are not there. Ever since you were a little child you never left my sight.

He steps down off the chest.

Dungu where are you? When you were young you were only interested in the past. (*He senses a change in himself.*) Dungu do you hear me? My voice has changed—become gruff. Today I've become a young man. When I talk my voice goes grrr, grrr, gruff. But I can't think whether to be happy or whether to be sad because you are not here—nowhere within reach of my voice. You have abandoned me, gone to the ends of the earth. Dungu …

Dungura tugs at the rope that goes from his shoulder through the middle of the audience and begins to pull it towards him. The rope falls in coils at his feet. He rolls on the ground and continues to tug at the rope. Finally, Dungu (mind and tied to the other end of the rope) enters through the main door at the back of the auditorium. He enters walking backwards and muttering about something happening far away in the distance.

DUNGURA: Dungu, where were you?

DUNGU: Do you hear the clock? The clock will continue to run for as long as it is wound. It runs for no particular purpose. It will run as long as the winding lasts.

DUNGURA: You don't know that I am now a young man. Can you feel the change?

DUNGU: I know you better than you can know yourself. Your voice is now cracked. That's why I decided to loaf around the town. I went from place to place just like the hands of the clock, from second to second. I didn't stay in one place.

DUNGURA: Where did you vanish the moment I fell asleep?

DUNGU: I went to savor life's briefest joy with the longest consequences.

DUNGURA: You could have taken me along.

DUNGU: The distances I travel in my mind you cannot go in your body. But we must fill up this sack. The time has come for you and me to walk together

DUNGURA: Is there nothing in the sack?

DUNGU: Not nothing—there is the hope that we can catch the first train.

Dungu pokes his head into the sack and peers. He then sits on the chest and ties the sack on his back. Dungura wears a tie around his neck.

Wasn't there a lamp here? Pick it up.

Dungura picks up the lamp that was stuck on a stick.

DUNGURA: This might be a lamp that someone left as an offering.

DUNGU: No, it was left to light us when we travel in the dark.

Dungu now climbs on the shoulders of Dungura.

If we hurry, we can catch the train.

(*while traveling*) What do you think about the two of us?

DUNGURA: I don't think about anything.

DUNGU: Good lord! I forgot! You can't think.

Dungu and Dungura step down from the stage. All the lights except the light of their lantern are extinguished. The light falls only on them.

DUNGU: It is too dark.

DUNGURA: The light of the lantern is not enough.

DUNGU: The lantern is trying to fill the space left by the absence of the sun. You're shivering aren't you?

DUNGURA: You're scared aren't you?

DUNGU: The footsteps of the men I met during the day sound very clear in the silence of the night.

DUNGURA: Think about something else.

DUNGU: I will think about our journey.

DUNGURA: There, now your shivering has stopped.

The two leave the stage.

Scene 2

There are two chairs placed beside the chest that was seen in Scene 1 and is meant to indicate a railway station. As the scene opens the sound of a train is heard and the train stops. Several different kinds of people and their loved ones are seen in the shadows of the darkened station. Dungura with Dungu on his back now come on stage from the right. The stage lights up with their entrance. One by one, the people get down and leave.

DUNGURA: A fair number of people have come back on this train.

DUNGU: I, for one, have no intention of coming back.

DUNGURA: The man who just got down from the train, why is he walking alone?

DUNGU: His mind is going in another direction—after a woman.

DUNGURA: Why is that huge man sitting on the shoulders of the little man?

DUNGU: The little man worships the big man. They are men who do not believe in themselves and so follow others.

As the last man climbs off the train, Dungu and Dungura climb on.

DUNGU: That last man who got off the train looks badly battered. His own mind is torturing him for wrongs he has committed.

DUNGURA: The train is moving forward.

DUNGU: I see the world as going backwards. Dungura, this train might go off the tracks.

DUNGURA: Nonsense.

DUNGU: I don't believe you. I'm scared.

DUNGURA: There's no way that can happen.

DUNGU: You may say that, but I don't believe it. I'm afraid.

Dungu puts his head out of the carriage and shouts to someone in front of the train.

DUNGU: Mr. Guard, sir, tell the engine driver that this train will go off the tracks.

DUNGURA: Even before the sun can kiss the earth people are awake. Where are they running in this dark?

DUNGU: They have got up early to start their struggle with life. They have no time to sit around and think, to be happy, to make love. Look at them. They don't have even a shadow of a thought. A clock ticks for no particular purpose. It keeps going for as long as it is wound.

DUNGURA: Today, too, the sun will rise.

DUNGU: Yes, the sun rises filling the heart with joy. At the end of the day the sun sets and the mind despairs.

DUNGURA: Men are running here and there. Their speed increases. Those who are running don't seem to see those who have fallen. They trample them as they run.

DUNGU: Those who are running have no intention of helping those who have fallen.

DUNGURA: People in the insane asylum have put up a board saying that everyone outside is mad.

DUNGU: Mosquitoes that sing a song in your ear and then suck your blood are everywhere.

DUNGURA: They have put up a sign on the main public road saying it is a private family burial ground.

DUNGU: Look! Look! Nero has come here, too, to play his fiddle.

DUNGURA: There's a man there at the edge of the road trying to find a little warmth.

DUNGU: The man is shivering. Is it really cold? (*to Dungura*) I see goose bumps on your body too. You are cold, Dungura. Just look away. I on my part will try to think of other things. That's a truly beastly act.

DUNGURA: Why do these people have their hands tied?

DUNGU: Because they write.

DUNGURA: Do they write obscenities?

DUNGU: They write about obscenities.

DUNGURA: Look the sun has risen even for the beggars.

DUNGU: Minds that can never be filled can in one instant fill stomachs that have never been filled. See how a back that could not bend down to give a beggar a coin, now bends to pick up a five cent piece fallen on the road.

DUNGURA: There's a meeting going on there.

DUNGU: A man is shouting at the top of his voice with his eyes closed. People listen with their fingers plugged in their ears. The eye sees what the mind cannot bear. The donkey does the work of the dog. The dog looks on with his eyes closed. The lizard has gold tied around its neck and is trying to fly. A frog has seen a tortoise and is dying to puff himself up to that size. The dog at the blacksmith's has been hit by lightning and he is still asleep. He sleeps with the fleas and the fleas blame the dog. Judges are in the witness box and the witnesses pronounce the verdicts. Men squirm in shame when they see people walking about naked. To be without shame is more powerful than being a king. They bite the hand that feeds them and then lick their lips. A mountain labors and brings forth a mouse and he tries to become an elephant. The land is mortgaged and he grins at the empty space. One man waits for another to die in so he can sell his coffins. When the tortoise is thrown into the water he shouts that he is drowning.

DUNGURA: Hey! That's the guy who is ruling the country—(*they both laugh*)

DUNGU: He climbs up—he climbs down—he shouts at the top of his voice—coughs—holds his chest and sits down—spit flows—snot flows—feces leak out.

They both laugh out loud.

DUNGURA: It's a good meditation on putrefaction. (*They laugh.*)

DUNGU: They are beating them.

DUNGURA: No they are throwing feces.

DUNGU: No they are bathing in feces. (*They laugh.*)

DUNGURA: It's like a pig's sty. The train has slowed down. The sun is setting.

DUNGU: People are running back. Their faces are despairing. There's not a smile on anyone's face.

DUNGURA: Perhaps people don't like the sun to set.

DUNGU: We will be on the train till the sun sets in the west. This is the first train from the station where we got on and the last train to the station where we get off.

DUNGURA: The train is about to stop.

DUNGU: There is not a soul around. The dead sleep soundly. The living are dead asleep.

Scene 3

The curtain backstage is lit by the rays of the morning sun. In the front of the stage on the two sides are two platforms. In the center of the stage as before is the big chest. In front of the back curtain and running across the stage is a long clothes line.

Chukkina (a woman's body) is on the left platform and is writhing in pain. Dungu and Dungura with their backs to each other are seated on the chest. Chukki (the woman's mind) comes on stage pushing an enormous sack, tries to get into it, then jumps out, looks at Chukkina and shouts.

DUNGURA: Why have you put your neck on a track where a train is not running? What are you waiting for?

CHUKKINA: I put my neck on a track where a train was running and very nearly got killed.

DUNGURA: Try calling on the gods.[1]

Chukkina searches for gods. She gets down off the chest.

DUNGURA: Who are you looking for?

CHUKKINA: For gods. (*She jumps out of the sack.*) Are you also looking for gods?

DUNGURA: I am looking for my expectations.

CHUKKINA: We, too, have looked for such things.

DUNGURA: I have so many questions

CHUKKINA: There are no answers.

CHUKKI: It is then one remembers God.

CHUKKINA: But God has still not come. Perhaps His Reverence has forgotten us or perhaps we have forgotten him. (*She is silent, thinking.*)

Dungura climbs up onto the platform.

CHUKKI: It's no use looking for God.

DUNGU: Are you that woman's mind?

CHUKKI: Yes, I am Chukkina's mind. Who was it who just spoke? Was it God?

DUNGU: No, it's me, Dungura's mind. Why did you ask us not to look for God?

CHUKKI: Do you think I don't have expectations?

DUNGU: Sure, you do.

CHUKKI: Right!

DUNGU: Do you think I don't have expectations?

CHUKKI: Sure you do.

DUNGU: That's right.

CHUKKI: I can't hate you for that.

DUNGU: Why don't you hate me?

CHUKKI: When the last train left there was not a single friend left, nor any enemies. There was no man left even to hate. I was completely alone. I waited for the morning train not in order to go anywhere. I wanted to push Chukkina on to the railway track and make an end to life. It is hard hanging onto life till dawn when one has no expectations. I searched for God, but His Reverence was not to be found. But now I do have an expectation and so I wish to live.

DUNGU: Is that an expectation about me?

CHUKKI: It could be …

DUNGU: Is it about love?

CHUKKI: It could be that.

DONGU: When you have feelings of love what do you think about me?

CHUKKI: I think you are the noblest man on earth.

DUNGU: That is how I think, too. People say you are a bad woman and come up with evidence to prove it. I argue with them and prove to them that you are a good woman.

CHUKKI: One's mind plays tricks on one
DUNGU: Do you imagine that love is pure?
CHUKKI: No. It is full of desire.
DUNGU: Shall we now share a chew of betel nut?
CHUKKI: Yes, let's.

Dungu, in the tradition of the folk plays, pounds the betel nut in the small mortar usually used for betel nut in a vulgar manner. Chukkina and Dungura stroke their backs with their own hands. It symbolizes sexual intercourse. Chukki and Dungu dance as if to the rhythm of a drum. The dance ends. Chukki and Dungu sit down languidly. Only their two figures are lit. Chikkuna and Dungura move to the back of the stage. Chukki and Dungu now climb back on to the seats.

DUNGU: The end of passion, dispassion, depression, is a sign of the birth of a child. We should have music playing on this occasion. But the past is something dead and gone, defunct.
CHUKKI: You may not know it but there is something from the past that still remains to influence the present.
DUNGU: The past is extinct.
CHUKKI: No, it regenerates.

A child crawls out from between Chukkina and Dungura from the back of the stage.

DUNGU: See! A renewal!
CHUKKI: Yes, a regeneration that was not extinguished by the past.
DUNGU: *(sees the child and says with pleasure)* A child!
CHUKKI: You are a father.

At this point, children's clothes and books should be displayed on stage.

DUNGU: Chukkino, nurse this child.
CHUKKI: Dungaro, make him big and strong.
DUNGU: We must give the child a name.
CHUKKI: Call him Mother's-son.
DUNGU: *(to the child)* Mother's-son, eat well and grow big and strong. Then when you grow up provide for your mother and father.
CHUKKI: *(to the child who is writing)* Mother's-son, study hard, learn to read and write. Then teach your mother.
DUNGU: Mother's-son, you will look after your mother and father won't you?
CHUKKI: Bless his heart! He surely will.

The child now comes on stage. Chukki and Dungu get down from the chairs and come towards him.

CHUKKI: What are you waiting for son? Go! Go out into the world.
DUNGU: Go, son. It is an endless desert out there with no road.

The child steps down from the stage and walks through the center of the auditorium to the back.

CHUKKI: You and I now have a world we can build.
DUNGU: You and I are now married.

Another child crawls out from the back of the stage.

FIRST CHILD: *(from the back of the auditorium)* Marriage is the union of two people. They fight to achieve their private desires, each in their own way. Marriage consists of conflict and fighting.
DUNGU: *(looking far out towards the back of the auditorium)* Good heavens! How high that little flea jumps!
CHUKKU: Dungu—another birth!
DUNGU: Another one?
CHUKKU: Yes, now you give him a name
DUNGU: Call him Father's-son
CHUKKI: Don't say the name when you think of your father.
DUNGU: Chukkino, nurse the baby.
CHUKKI: Dunguro, help him to grow big and strong.

Chukkina and Dungura nurse the child, feed him and make him grow big and strong.

DUNGU: When we make him big and strong what becomes of us the parents?
CHUKKI: They grow old.
DUNGU: Will our children care for us in our old age?
CHUKKI: How can they not? They are our children.

FATHER'S-SON: *(dances)*

thana thana thaka ya tith theka
tho kaya dada debila katha thathana

The child comes to the front of the stage. Dungu and Chiukku go to him.

DUNGU: All that your father could not do, you must do.
CHUKKI: Father's-son, don't add anything special to your name.
DUNGU: Go forth. Keep going until your nose hits the ground and your rear end goes up.
CHUKKI: Keep in mind. We must build a house that we can call our own.

Father's-son steps down from the stage and as he walks thorough the auditorium he preaches to the parents on intelligence. A third child crawls on stage while a fourth peeps from behind the curtain.

FATHER'S-SON: Houses exist. We have seen them. (*Then he turns back and asks*) But in reality, do houses exist?

Chukku and Dungu look at him astounded.

A house is made up of numerous parts. Those parts can be broken up into smaller and smaller parts. The small parts can be further subdivided into yet smaller and smaller parts. Division keeps on until it arrives at the atom. A house is a collection of atoms. An atom is not a solid object. Nor is it something else. It is a constant motion. There is no such thing as a house. That is a complete falsehood.

DUNGU: That fellow is going to do the kind of job even his father's father could not do.

CHUKKI: Dungu—another birth!

DUNGU: Good heavens woman! Don't you have anything else to do?!

CHUKKI: He is your child too.

DUNGU: I can't believe it is mine.

CHUKKI: Aren't you going to name him?

DUNGU: No point. The neighbors will give him a name.

Chukki and Dungu dress him up as a dancer and give him a book. The child begins to dance.

DUNGU: The book the fellow is reading is not anything we have read.

CHUKKI: Do what even your grandfather and great grandfather did not do.

DUNGU: Don't forget your parents.

CHUKKI: The road is long and very tiring. Take care.

When Dancer-Boy leaves the stage Monkey-Boy enters. He falls asleep on the chest. He is woken up and given a book, but he falls asleep again in the middle of the stage.

CHUKKI: Wake up little Monkey-Boy. Open your big eyes. Look far ahead and go.

When Monkey-Boy leaves the stage Thinking-Girl comes forward.

DUNGU: It is good to think.

CHUKKI: But one must think about what it is one thinks.

When she leaves the stage Disabled-Boy enters.

DUNGU: Consider this not just your fate. Make it your heritage.

When he leaves Premature-Boy enters and walks off the stage swaying as if he were floating.

CHUKKI: He couldn't wait the ten months—impatient fellow.

DUNGU: Robotic children!

CHUKKI: Robotic parents!

DUNGU: If a great number of drops collect together will it form one digit?
CHUKKI: If a large number of children gather will they create a future?

The children all leave. Dungura and Chukkina sit on the chairs. Dungu and Chukki climb on to the chest. They are alone on stage.

DUNGU: Births are now over, extinct.
CHUKKI: But expectations are not extinct.
DUNGU: Will our children care for us?
CHUKKI: Like all parents we, too, will gaze far into the distance and wait anxiously for our children's return.
DUNGU: We now need a little leisure in our lives.
CHUKKI: Someday they will come looking for us.
DUNGU: Till then we will wait anxiously watching the road.

Scene 4

The stage set for Scene 4 remains the same. Chukkina and Dungura are now old. They have waited for years for their children's return. Everything is quiet. Only the ticking of the clock is heard. Dungu seated in the middle of the stage, stands up, looks long and far into the distance and then when all hope is shattered returns and sits down. Chukki, too, walks to the front of the stage, looks long into the distance and as hopes fail comes back and sits down.

DUNGU: The children have still not come.
CHUKKI: I'm beginning to think that they've forgotten us.
DUNGU: That's a terrible thing to say—an unbearable thought.
CHUKKI: Do you hear the clock tick? Short sound—long sound. The short sound is like the moments of pain in our lives. The long sound is life's boredom. You and I, like the ticking of the clock swing back and forth between boredom and pain.

Dungura gets off his seat and comes up to Dungu.

DUNGURA: Dungu, my back aches.
CHUKKINA: *(from her seat)* Chukki, I feel numbness in my limbs.
CHUKKI: You are old.
DUNGURA: Can't you rub some oil on my back?
DUNGU: The two of you see to each other's welfare.

Dungu and Chukki place Dungura's and Chukkina's chairs close to each other.

CHUKKI: There now. Rub the oil and massage each other.

Dungura gets back onto his seat. Chukkina and Dungura medicate and massage each other.

DUNGU: (*to Chukki*) What do you think has become of our children? What would they now be?

CHUKKI: I think Mother's-son must be now a teacher.

DUNGU: Father's-son must be a doctor.

CHUKKI: You remember the one who was big and strong?

DUNGU: He must be a fireman.

CHUKKI: What about the one who didn't sleep and cried all night?

DUNGU: He must be a security guard. Remember the one who couldn't fall asleep until he pinched someone?

CHUKKI: He must be a prison guard maintaining law and order.

DUNGU: There was the one who caused a riot demanding mother's milk.

CHUKKI: He must be a worker.

DUNGU: What about the one who was no good at anything–all he had was a big mouth?

CHUKKI: He must surely be a politician.

DUNGU: And the one who had visions of building a new world?

CHUKKI: He must be long dead now.

CHUKKINA: You said you had a backache.

DUNGURA: Who said I had no backbone? Look how nicely it is bent. You said your breasts were numb.

CHUKKINA: My breasts have long been dry. No milk. No young ones to nurse. By now you must be about the age of two donkeys from Puttalam[2]

DUNGURA: Punnakku?[3] Cattle feed? If we ate the *punnakku* they give to cattle we would be much stronger now. Its's not eating *punnakku* that is our problem.

CHUKKINA: Can you kiss me?

DUNGURA: I can't kiss you in unmentionable places.

CHUKKINA: Kiss my face.

DUNGURA: That is all wrinkled.

CHUKKINA: What a shame. It was such a pretty face. That means you can't kiss me.

DUNGURA: To kiss you I have to unbend my back.

CHUKKINA: Shall I rub a little oil on it?

DUNGURA: Where?

CHUKKINA: On your back.

Chukkina rubs oil on Dungura's back.

DUNGURA: Enough enough! Uh … uh …. Uh …. Stop it, you bitch. I nearly used the four-letter word.

CHUKKINA: Why do you struggle? Keep still.

DUNGURA: Dungu look! This woman is clawing me.

CHUKKI: The soft attractions of youth disappear with age.

CHUKKINA: Chukki see what he did. The medicinal oil I got for the wound on my hand he poured it all over my head.

Dungura sneezes.

DUNGU: Your children are thinking of you.

CHUKKI: A sneeze is only an expectation.

CHUKKINA: Chukki, look! There's snot dripping from this old fellow's nose.

DUNGURA: When I ask for coriander water for my cold, this woman forces me to drink Penela leaf concoctions.[4]

DUNGU: You two are about to die and enter your next birth.

CHUKKI: Our hopes of the children are now fading.

DUNGU: Why do you keep thinking of the children and suffering?

CHUKKI: I enjoy the pleasure from pain more than the pleasure from happiness.

DUNGU: Yes, happiness is ephemeral. Pain is permanent.

CHUKKI: Our minds no longer have the ability to derive pleasure from pain or pleasure from happiness.

DUNGU: They won't come. Some day they, too, will learn the pain of expectation.

CHUKKI: I will plead with the gods not to shatter my hopes.

DUNGU: Yes, create ever more expectations. I for one am going back to my birthplace.

CHUKKI: I who was born in the streets can create no more expectations. I am going to search for God.

Dungura gets off his seat. Dungu climbs on Dungura's back. Dungura picks up the stick with the lantern and they begin their journey. Dungura whimpers.

DUNGU: Am I too heavy for you?

DUNGURA: No.

DUNGU: Then why do you whimper?

DUNGURA: It is a bit of a weight.

DUNGU: Would it be better if you eased your load?

DUNGURA: No matter. The weight on my back makes me forget the weight on my mind.

Dungu and Dungura leave the stage.

CHUKKI: (*looks for her god*) Where is our God? What happened to him?

CHUKKINA: I'm lonely.

CHUKKI: I'm looking for my God. Where has His Worship gone?

CHUKKINA: I'm lonely.

CHUKKI: (*In pain—her last hope dashed.*) Our god is dead. Who killed His Reverence?

CHUKKINA: I'm lonely.

CHUKKI: We are the murderers. We have no God.

CHUKKINA: Lonely …

CHUKKI: We are destitute. There's no refuge—a world without gods. Where can we find answers to questions that have no answers? The whole world is empty.

CHUKKINA: I can't bear the loneliness.
CHUKKI: There's only one thing to do—to die.
CHUKKINA: Die?
CHUKKI: Yes. Take one's life.
CHUKKINA: That I can't do.
CHUKKI: Not alone, you can't.

Chukki puts her feet into the sack and stretches out her arms and squeezes Cukkina's neck. Chukkina allows it.

CHUKKI: The mind should control the body

One should envy oneself.
One should hate oneself.
There should be nothing one cannot do.
There must be no pain that the mind cannot bear.

The mind becomes strong and supreme.

The mind must be strong
The mind must be evil
to reach the highest point of cruelty in a man's mind,
the highest point of cruelty,
the highest point of cruelty,
the cruel mind's supreme place.

Chukkina struggles, whimpers and falls silent. Chukki climbs into the sack and disappears.

A collection of children holding black umbrellas come on stage. They stand around the chest where Chukkina sat and burst into sobs. Chukki puts her head out of the sack.

CHUKKI: Your mother is dead. You should have cried when she was alive. Now be happy. She had no treasure left to give you.

The children's sobs stop. One by one they slowly leave the stage.

CHUKKI: When a person dies people weep not out of grief at the death. They weep because they do not get the things they expected to get. Else every man should shed a tear for every person who is found dead on the street. No one sheds tears for another. To weep for another is a lie.

The children all cover their faces with their umbrellas and walk out through the middle of the auditorium. Musicians fill in the time between the scenes. Chukki pokes her head back inside the sack.

Scene 5

The stage is set as it was in Scene 1. It is Dungura's birthplace. While the window and the large chest are just as they were before, they are now dilapidated and in a state of decay. Dungura now riding on the back of Dungu enters the birthing room. Chukki mutters something from inside.

CHUKKI: Dungu, don't worry your head about anything. Let whatever has to happen, happen. When you feel like laughing laugh. When you feel like crying cry. If you want to walk, walk. When you want to sit down, sit down. Have no hopes or expectations about anything that exists or does not exist. Take your mind off all ideas of good and bad. Grief, joy, birth death, desire, disgust, likes, dislikes, hate, love, these are not emotions we need to endure anymore. Take refuge only in yourself.

Dungu and Dungura come on stage. Chukki leaves. Dungura carries a stick and a lantern. Dungu has a sack on his back.

DUNGU: Not bad, that ride on my back!
DUNGURA: When I was young and able you rode on my back. (*Dungura gets down.*) Isn't this the place from which we started?
DUNGU: (*in a whisper*) This must also be the terminus.

Dungu peers inside the chest.

DUNGURA: What's inside that chest?
DUNGU: The treasures of generations.
DUNGURA: (*looking inside the chest*) There's not a damn thing inside.
DUNGU: It's a good thing there is nothing left.
DUNGURA: Mother and father must have taken everything when they left.
DUNGU: They didn't take anything.
DUNGURA: Perhaps then the grandparents and great grandparents did.
DUNGU: They too left empty-handed.

Dungu places the sack on the ground. Dungura hangs the lantern back on its hook.

DUNGURA: What's in that sack?
DUNGU: What was in it has fallen off along the way.
DUNGURA: Why? Just like sugar hidden under a dam!
DUNGU: Yes, all dissolved and gone.
DUNGURA: Just like frogs collected in a three-sided box!
DUNGU: Yes, all escaped.
DUNGURA: Like the bull buried in the earth.

DUNGU: Rotted.

DUNGURA: Like objects left for safe keeping.

DUNGU: Decayed.

DUNGU: Climb into your chest.

DUNGURA: My great-great-great-great-grand father gave this chest to my great-great-great-grand father. My great-great-great-grandfather gave it to my great-great-grandfather. My great-great grandfather gave it to my great grandfather. My great-grandfather gave it to my grandfather who gave it to father who gave it to me.

DUNGU: Whom do you have to leave it to?

DUNGURA: (*climbing into his room*) I remember how as a child I climbed into this.

DUNGU: You are back to your childhood—ready for your next birth!

DUNGURA: Dungu, can you see what time it is on the clock?

DUNGU: (*goes to the window*) There's a huge crowd by the clock tower. People are protesting that twenty-four hours in a day are not enough.

DUNGURRA: As for me even 12 hours are too much.

DUNGU: They are all small men trying to be big men.

DUNGURA: I asked you what time it was.

DUNGU: (*looking out through the window*) That man got up before cock crow, washed his mouth with a sip of tea; lingered in the toilet until the water slowly filled the bucket; buttoned his last trouser button only at the station. The train, packed solid, releases unseemly desires. A hip is touched and obscene words hit back at him. The man is now aroused. The machine moves faster than the clock. The man works faster than the machine. The machine stops. The man continues working. He gets caught in the rain so has his bath along the way. He arrives home just as the lamps are snuffed. He wants to enjoy his child's prattle. The child is asleep. He wishes to make love to his woman, but she is asleep. He cannot fall asleep, so he changes his pillow. He can't sleep. His mind works all night.

DUNGURA: It must be about six on the clock tower.

DUNGU: Whatever the time may be it is always six on that clock's face.

DUNGURA: Is it six in the morning or six in the evening?

DUNGU: Hard to say. The clock is right. There is nothing now left to add to our lives. Today there is no difference between us and the clock Dungura.

Dungu stares out of the window and begins to sob.

DUNGURA: What are you looking at?

DUNGU: What I can't help looking at.

DUNGURA: Why are you crying? For whom are you crying?

DUNGU: I have no unselfish thought that can bring a tear to my eye on behalf of another. Look at what the world is like. It's like a carnival. Among thousands of people you and I are alone.

Dungu moves away from the window and comes towards the chest.

We cannot now join in their pleasures. We do not have the language to respond to their talk. Our grammar is outdated. We cannot walk along with them our shoes are not strong enough. We cannot smile or join in their laughter. We don't have enough teeth in our mouth. The old are a race put in a corner. We are old. They don't know that though the body is old the mind still has its animal lusts and desires.

All we old ones can do now is to think about those things and moan for ourselves, think about those things and feel envious. How can I calm my mind? I forget who I am. I have forgotten myself.

Dungu climbs up near the window.

Let him go you idiot. Let him fall. Let him experience loneliness like me.

DUNGURA: Whom are you shouting at?
DUNGU: Two children are dragging their father.
DUNGURA: Where to?
DUNGU: To the old people's home. We don't have children even to discard us.
DUNGURA: To whom do we belong?
DUNGU: We ourselves don't know to whom we belong.
DUNGURA: We belong to ourselves.
DUNGU: What's wrong is that it isn't so. Look at those young chicks and young bucks holding hands and walking along the road. I can't bear to see them. They laugh. I can't control my rage. Do something to me. At least you do something. Hit me.
DUNGURA: Its our past, their future.
DUNGU: Our present is their future. I'll be glad when they too become old fossils like us. I can't wait to see that.
DUNGURA: That doesn't bother me.
DUNGU: You are old. That world has no value for you. I still desire that world. We must go back there. Climb on my back. Let's go.
DUNGURA: I can't. I have no strength left in my body.
DUNGU: When the body has no strength, we must go even if it's only with the strength of our minds.
DUNGURA: Can't you see? I'm an old man.
DUNGU: I won't sacrifice my pleasure for your old age.
DUNGURA: The world will laugh at us.
DUNGU: I won't sacrifice my desire for the sake of morality. Climb on my back. What are you waiting for?

Dungu backs towards the chest, lowers his head and shouts.

Climb on my back you idiot. Climb on without making an animal of me, your mind.

Dungura climbs on to Dungu's back. The lid of the box comes down on Dungu's neck.

Get down you old fool. I cannot go on this journey with you.

Dungu drops Dungura on to the floor, goes to the lamp, takes it in both hands and very carefully gets down off the stage. Stepping quietly, he goes into the midst of the audience. He looks around at the audience with his light. He is scared. Terribly afraid he shivers. Quickly he goes back to Dungura.

DUNGU: Dunguro.[5] Death is not frightening. But to live is terribly frightening.

Dungu opens the lid of the chest and Dungura climbs in.

Dunguro go disappear so that only your mind can see you. Hide so no one else can see you.

Dungu now takes the lamp and timidly climbs up to the window.

DUNGU: Dunguro, the world is not so bad. There's a place in it for the old. Look it's the old ones who go for the most parties and dances.

DUNGURA: (*from inside the chest*) If you my mind did not slide after beautiful things, I would not see anything. If you did not crawl after sounds I would hear nothing. If you did not run after scents and perfumes I would not sense anything. In order to end this, let us agree on a single goal.

Dungu climbs on the chest and looks at Dunguro who is inside.

DUNGU: Hey, you! Look how the cats are practicing moral behavior. How about you? Aren't you practicing the five precepts?[6] Let it be Dunguro. There's no morality left in the world for you and me.

Dungu takes the lamp and climbs back to the window.

DUNGU: What time did you say it was just now?

DUNGURA: Six o'clock.

DUNGU: The time is right. It will soon be the right time for us too. The sun is setting. Bubbles of light appear here and there.

DUNGURA: That may be why I can't see you.

DUNGU: It's not that dark.

DUNGURA: My entire body is trembling. Come here. Come and get inside this chest.

DUNGU: Don't be afraid. The sun will rise again tomorrow.

DUNGURA: Do you really believe that? Let's make up our minds that it will be so. You and I were born here in this empty room. Now you and I are again in this empty room.

DUNGU: We are now nearing our next birth. We begin life alone and will end life alone.

DUNGURA: I can't see anything. The darkness is trying to scare me. Why don't you put some oil into that lamp?

DUNGU: We don't have so much as a penny's worth of oil left.

DUNGURA: My entire body is numb. Can you see me?

DUNGU: I can't accept this life. We still have a lot of rights and responsibilities. We don't have one single person left whose duty it is to give you even a drop of water at this moment, Dunguro.

DUNGURO: Dungu, why are you silent? Why don't you at least talk to me. Don't you hear what I say? There is not a sound. Is the whole world gone dumb? Have I gone deaf?

DUNGU: It doesn't matter, Dunguro. Even though there is no one to give us what is our due we still have duties to perform.

Dungu slowly walks into the middle of the audience. He looks at everyone. His eyes are full of tears.

DUNGU: All we have left is this large chest. It belongs to all.

Realizing that the light of his lamp is flickering Dungu alarmed climbs back on stage.

DUNGU: The light of the lamp is almost gone.

He picks up the lamp and brings it to the middle of the stage and puts it down there.

DUNGU: The lamp is about to go out … We cannot allow it. I want light for all time. I cannot get lost in the dark. He raises the wick but the light dims. Dunguro, it is not like it was before. The more I try to increase the light the dimmer the light becomes. (*looks around*) Dunguro it is not just you. I too am afraid. But I can't see where you are. (*stares at the light*)

Light, light up my life.
The dark is a collected breath.
It's a life that does not meet the eye
A body that cannot feel a breath
A whimper not heard by the ear
Give me light … give me light!

Dunguro the light has gone out.
Why don't you talk?
I want to come to you.
We must agree on a single goal. I cannot see anything.
You have left me.
I delayed coming to you.
Like the second hand of a clock going from moment to moment from place to place throughout my entire life I have gone round in the same circle. I have

been unable to go beyond it. Life is not a truth. It is only a dream.
The sun is not going to shine again on your world.
The sun will not shine again on your world.
The sun will not shine again on your world.
The sun will not shine again on your world.
Dungu climbs into the sack and disappears.

Scene 6

When the empty stage lights up two sacks move to the front of the stage. Dungu puts his head out of the first sack and speaks.

DUNGU:

I have gone to hell
Everyone looks on
Hell does not have the anticipated tortures and pain
It is not difficult to understand that
Because we suffered before we got to hell.

CHUKKI:

I went in search of heaven
Unable to understand happiness and joy my life was aborted
The joys and pleasures I expected are not there
Heaven cannot make life happy.

DUNGU: There is no end. (*The light on the sacks fades.*)
asatō mā sadgamaya (lead me from falsehood to truth)
tamasō mā jeyātitargamaya (lead me from darkness to light)
mā tamā amaram gamaya (lead me from death to the deathless)

The curtain falls.

The end

****

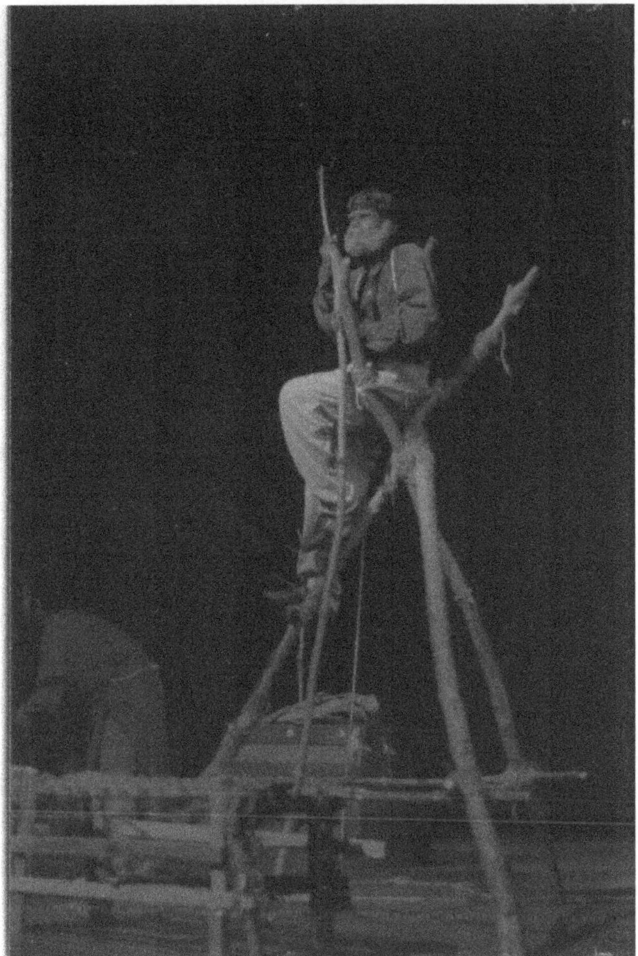

PHOTOGRAPH 4.1 Dungura in *Shadows and Men*. Photograph courtesy of Prasanna Jayakody

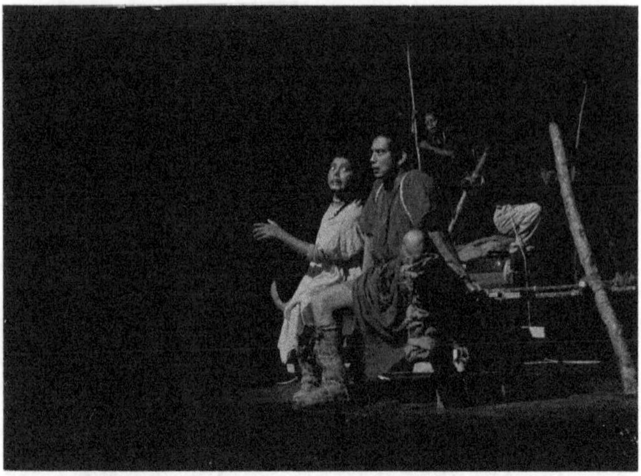

PHOTOGRAPH 4.2 Dungu and Chukki in *Shadows and Men*. Photograph courtesy of Prasanna Jayakody

Notes

1 Several of the Hindu gods have been incorporated to the Buddhist pantheon and people turn to them in times of distress.
2 Wild donkeys from the region of Puttlam are said to live to a ripe old age.
3 *Punnakku* is a kind of meal made from coconut and other grains that is fed to cattle. Dungura mishears *Punnakku* for Puttalam.
4 Corriander is a traditional medicine given for colds. Penala leaf concoctions are considered to increase men's sexual potency.
5 When addressing a person affectionately, one tends to use this form.
6 The five precepts in Buddhism are as follows: I will not kill, I will not take what belongs to others, I will not indulge in sexual misconduct, I will refrain from wrong speech and lies and I will refrain from taking intoxicants. These are the fundamental precepts that Buddhist are expected to observe.

***

Prasanna Jayakody, better known today as a film maker than a theater director, created *Shadows and Men* in 1993. It is his first and only play. His play is a meditation on life and we find similar attempts in his films such as *Sankara* (2007), *Karma* (2010), *28* (2014) and *Sansare Dadayakkaraya/Leopard Do Not Bite* (2015), which explore themes related to sexuality, desire, life and death. His films are known for their striking visual imagery and compositions. Prasanna's films have won several awards in international film festivals including for directing *Sankara* at the Cairo International Festival in 2007; *28* was named the Best Asian Film at the Amsterdam Film Awards in 2014. His artistic gaze is informed by the social, psychological and philosophical terrain around him.

AREN'T YOU GOING TO SHOOT ME? (MATA VEḌITIYANNÄDDA? 1999)

Rajitha Dissanayake

Characters

UPUL—Age 23. Looks energetic and attractive. He does not have a permanent job and is a member of a Calypso band that sings at restaurants. Often seen in a pair of jeans and t-shirt with a long-sleeve shirt folded up to the elbows and shoes. Sometimes wears a tucked in long-sleeve shirt or a t-shirt. Wears a skinny top when in the room.

RAVI—Age 22. University student. Seems very reserved. He is financially dependent on his parents and seems to have the parents' attention. Often seen in a pair of jeans, short-sleeve shirt and collarless t-shirt. Wears a white vest when in the room.

DRIVER—Age 27. Seen in trousers and shirt untucked. Seems submissive.

LAND LORD—Age 40. Seen in trousers, long-sleeve untucked black shirt and shoes.

THE MAN FROM UPSTAIRS—Age 45. Seen in black trousers, long-sleeve untucked white shirt and shoes.

INDIRA—Looks to be about 25 years of age. Seen in pants, kurta top and slippers.

DHAMMI—Looks to be about 22 years of age. Seen in a blue knee-length dress and heels.

CALYPSO BAND—Seen in denims, white long-sleeve shirts folded up to the elbows and shoes.

A room with a table, two chairs and two beds. Ravi sits on a bed and gazes out of the window at something outside. Below the stage a group of musicians play. Upul, one of the musicians, sings in a loud voice:

If one can only see but cannot experience
Is that enough I ask?

What kind of answer will someone give?
If someone were to ask
Why I so want to know?
Even if I could manage an answer
It is unlikely he'll not ask me another.
Can language enable us to understand life?

The music stops. Upul carrying a guitar climbs onto the stage, walks across and disappears. Two other musicians leave. Ravi stretches out on the bed and shakes a leg. Upul enters the room carrying a box of books, a bag and his guitar.

UPUL: Good morning my good friend. What news? How are things? Do you like this place?

Upul puts the box down and places his bag and guitar on the table.

I finished early today. I was scared it would be dark and I wouldn't be able to find the bus stop for this place.

Upul sits on the other bed and takes off his shoes. Ravi sits up on his bed looks at something outside the window and turns to Upul.

RAVI: I'm very glad there is a window here.

Upul stretches out on his bed and lifts his legs doing his exercises.

RAVI: I said it was a good thing there was a window here. I can sit here now for any length of time.

UPUL: What do you say? Shall we start running from tomorrow?

RAVI: I've been thinking I'll start to meditate.

UPUL: Meditation is also good, but one must keep the body fit.

RAVI: Though I said at first that this room was OK do you know I really didn't like it at all. I agreed to it only because we had to leave the other place and couldn't find any other.

UPUL: Before one can decide on what is good or bad about this place one must at least stay a week.

RAVI: It doesn't seem such a bad place. We might even stay here for ever.

Upul takes a few sips of water from a bottle on the table.

UPUL: When I was in the bus this morning I saw your university students carrying placards and shouting along the road.

Ravi puts the box of books on a chair and arranges the books on the table. Upul sits on the bed and brushes his shoes.

RAVI: Can you imagine the kind of feelings one experiences when one sees two lovely legs stepping gracefully to music?

UPUL: I don't know about stepping to music, I can barely keep my back straight. My whole body is aching after carrying your load of books. What is that pile of books worth?

RAVI: Here, I have books from the *Sasadavata*[1] to the postmodern …
UPUL: I asked you their value in rupees.
RAVI: You took two of my books the other day didn't you?
UPUL: I'll get them back.
RAVI: To whom did you give them?
UPUL: I'll get them back.

Upul takes out a few shirts and trousers from his bag, then puts them back in.

RAVI: When are you going home?
UPUL: Mother sent a letter again yesterday.
RAVI: When do you go?
UPUL: If you don't go home once in two weeks your father comes tearing in here the very next day. Don't you find that a nuisance?
RAVI: My mother is very scared that something terrible will happen to me.
UPUL: My family waits till I come in the hope of getting relief from their troubles. Folks at home imagine that I live a very comfortable life here.
RAVI: You know something! The landlord wanted to know if he was to ask the milkman to deliver milk for us each morning!
UPUL: What did you tell him?
RAVI: I didn't tell him that we only drank plain tea.
UPUL: So, did you say, yes?
RAVI: Yes, let's have a glass of milk each morning like we used to do at home. However, when he asked whether we wanted the newspapers delivered I told him that you get yours at the office and that I read mine at the library.
UPUL: What a pity!
RAVI: Why …
UPUL: Since we don't have many such people visiting us here we should have asked the newspaper delivery man to come too!

Ravi sits on a chair and begins to turn the pages of a book.

RAVI: When do you get your pay?
UPUL: What pay?
RAVI: Aren't you likely to get a lucky break one of these days?
UPUL: If my job gets set tomorrow, I will return the money I borrowed from you.

Upul takes a paper cone of roasted gram,[2] sits on the table and eats.

UPUL: Aren't there more mosquitoes here than in the last place we lived?
RAVI: We must ask the landlord to spray mosquito repellent on that drain outside.

Upul hands the cone of gram to Ravi who puts a few in his mouth and goes back to his book.

UPUL: If one could be the owner of a room like this, one would have some money coming in even if one did nothing.

Upul opens out the paper cone and begins to read.

Don't you like to read old newspapers? This one says that there are beings yet to be born who are capable of doing even worse things. Look here are some great facts. Just read it. See for yourself.

Upul gives Ravi the piece of paper, takes his towel and leaves the room. Ravi goes to the window and stares at something outside. Upul returns drying himself. Ravi sits on his bed.

UPUL: If our team wins this time I'm going to throw a party. What do you say? True, there's a chance they may lose. Isn't that so? Those fellows throw the ball straight at our guys' legs.

RAVI: If the legs are so lovely can the face not be so too?

Upul takes a comb from his bag and combs his hair.

RAVI: What part of the body do you like most?

UPUL: Whose? Mine?

RAVI: No. Anybody's.

UPUL: If it's yours—I dislike most your mouth.

Silence.

RAVI: Do you think the color of her complexion can change with the light? Everything looks beautiful when moon light falls through the trees.

UPUL: Shut that window. I'm cold. Mosquitoes can get in.

Upul tears a page off one of the books on the table, sits on a chair and begins to write. Ravi walks to the table and looks at the book from which Upul tore the page.

UPUL: Did I tell you about my new girl? I gave her a song I wrote for her. You know what she said? She asked me to write another for her and bring it tomorrow. In the rush I forgot to call Dhammi today. Tomorrow, when I see her she'll glower at me.

Upul writes something on the paper. Ravi stands by the table looking at him.

RAVI: From what part of a person's body can one tell a person's nature? What part must one see in order to fall in love? I ask you, must one see the whole body?

Silence.

RAVI: By looking just at a person's legs what can one know about the person?

UPUL: You know don't you, when I first saw a woman?

RAVI: I don't remember.

UPUL: That's strange! I told you about it so many times, but you don't seem to remember the story. Wait. Let me finish what I'm doing.

Upul continues to write and Ravi looks on.

RAVI: In order to tell whether a woman is beautiful what part of her must one see?
UPUL: Any healthy clean woman is beautiful. However, just as what one sees by moonlight changes when seen in the daylight, so it is once one begins to associate with a person.
RAVI: Not everybody will be like that.
UPUL: How's that?
RAVI: I said everybody won't be like that.
UPUL: About whom are you talking?
RAVI: Nobody in particular.
UPUL: Then?
RAVI: Just a thought.
UPUL: Since when is this? Why have you not told me?
RAVI: What?

Ravi sits on the bed hugs his pillow and smiles at Upul.

UPUL: Is it someone around here? What's her name? Is she pretty?

Upul walks up to Ravi and hugs him.

Need any help?

Ravi cringes in embarrassment. He pushes Upul aside, takes his towel and walks out of the room.

UPUL: Be careful when you open that tap in the toilet. The water comes gushing out.

Upul takes up his guitar and begins to strum, singing softly. The stage lights go out. When the stage lights up again Ravi is on his bed in a meditative posture with his back to the window. Upul wearing a tie and shoes enters carrying a bag.

UPUL: Why so early today? Didn't you go out? Didn't you even go to the library?

Upul places his bag on the table and loosens his tie.

If you checked the new gazette notifications you could send in one or two job applications next week.

Upul sits on Ravi's bed and takes his shoes off.

UPUL: Did you know that a bomb went off near the clock tower today? Many died, they say. In the middle of all that our guys have lost the game. There is a rumor that tomorrow the buses are going on strike.

Upul keeps his shoes beside his bed. He cleans out his wallet and throws out the unnecessary papers onto the floor.

UPUL: Shall I fix that job at the video club for you? The time when you could answer loud and clear that you were a university student, when someone asked what you did, is now long past, vanished imperceptibly.[3] You've been luckier than me by four years.

Silence.

You know what? I've a new job from tomorrow – to sing at a club. I get a free dinner too. I'll find out when I go there tomorrow if I can take you along. Even if you can't sing, if you can talk the kind of talk that floods people's minds with happiness, that would be great.

Upul goes up to Ravi.

On this lovely, serene evening let us all raise our hands and applaud and in order to experience how beautiful life is let us sing a lovely song and all join in a dance.

Upul slaps Ravi on the back. Ravi's meditation shatters.

UPUL: What do you say to that? However, it's only when one has to stay up till two and three in the morning every night that it hits you the next day.

Upul sits on the table and takes up his guitar. Ravi turns to the window and stares at something outside.

UPUL: (*sings*)

Show me the way to find you
I have no one
Every night without you
Is torment
I wait for the sun to rise again.
Where will I see you?
On the pavement, in a bus, or the train,
At Majestic city or on Galle Road
Where will I meet you?
Show me the way to find you
I have no one.

Upul looks at Ravi who is staring at something outside the window. Upul takes out a paper cone filled with roasted gram from his bag.

UPUL: What are you doing seated by that window? What are you staring at?
RAVI: Nothing.

Ravi turns to Upul and then looks down. Upul walks to Ravi, gives him the cone of gram and stands by the window.

UPUL: What a stunningly beautiful sight! You are a very nasty man. Why didn't you show this to me earlier?

RAVI: What?

UPUL: What a beauty. It's a shame we can see only her legs. I think she's less than 20. She walks back and forth so rhythmically as if she were singing a song.

Ravi sits by the table.

RAVI: Do you know who lives on the ground floor of that house?

UPUL: Who?

RAVI: It must be her daughter.

UPUL: Whose daughter?

Ravi picks up the piece of paper on the table and reads.

RAVI: You've written saying you are suffering. To whom?

UPUL: To my mother.

RAVI: Is your mother's name Suddi?

UPUL: Stop reading other people's letters.

Upul goes to the window. Ravi stares at him. Upul comes to Ravi and puts on his slippers.

UPUL: I'm going outside for a short walk.

Upul leaves. Ravi takes up the books on the table one by one and then puts each back again. Lights go off on stage.

The stage lights come on. Upul is asleep on his bed. Ravi enters with a few books in his hand. He puts them on the table, takes off his shirt and sits on his bed. Upul gets up and moves to the window, then returns to the table, sits down and takes a few sips of water from a bottle.

UPUL: There was a letter here. Where is it? I'm asking you where is the letter that was here yesterday?

RAVI: Whose letter?

UPUL: Is there anyone else here other than the two of us?

RAVI: I don't know

UPUL: What don't you know?

RAVI: The letter.

UPUL: So?

RAVI: It has nothing to do with me.

UPUL: Then why did you read it yesterday?

RAVI: I've told you once now …
UPUL: I asked why the hell did you read it?
RAVI: I didn't read any damn thing.
UPUL: Then?
RAVI: There was a letter on the table.
UPUL: So?
RAVI: That's all.
UPUL: How can that be all?

Upul ruffles through the books on the table.

Ravi please … (*he finds the letter*) Who put it among these books?

Upul reads the letter smiling to himself.

Do you know to whom I intend to send this letter?

Silence.

To write a love letter to one person and be able to give it to someone else—Isn't that something?

RAVI: That is of no interest to me.
UPUL: Why do you say that? What then does interest you?

Silence.

UPUL: Why? What's the problem? If you have a problem, tell me. If I have a problem I'll tell you. Or do you expect me to confide in the landlord?
RAVI: Go tell it to that woman upstairs.
UPUL: You know, I am planning to tell her.
RAVI: What?
UPUL: Everything.

Silence.

RAVI: What were you planning to tell that girl?
UPUL: What girl?
RAVI: The one you just mentioned.
UPUL: Ah … her. Do you know who her husband is?
RAVI: Husband?

Upul walks to the window.

UPUL: Hey Ravi my boy! Look! Having a window here in this room makes all the difference. Any qualms I had about paying the extra100 rupees for this place have all vanished.

Ravi arranges the books on the table.

RAVI: None of that matters to me.
UPUL: Why do you say that?
RAVI: Because it doesn't matter to me.
UPUL: How come?

Ravi packs his clothes into a bag.

RAVI: Because I'm going home tomorrow.
UPUL: You said you weren't going home till after next week.
RAVI: I must look for a better place.
UPUL: For whom?
RAVI: For me.
UPUL: Why?
RAVI: Because I want to find a better place.
UPUL: Why what's your problem with this? We should at least wait a week before deciding whether it is good or bad. Besides, I just heard you say you could stay here for ever.

Silence.

After tramping the streets all day trying to earn a pittance to survive it is such a relief to get to this room and stand by this window. It makes all the tiredness go away.

RAVI: I'm going out.
UPUL: Yes, take a walk and be back. There's a friend coming over this evening.
RAVI: Who?
UPUL: Go where you want. I'll introduce you when you get back.

Ravi leaves. Upul stretches out on the bed. He sings a song under his breath. There is a knock on the door. Upul starts up.

UPUL: Come in. Come right in.

The driver enters. He sits in a chair by the table. Upul sits on the bed.

UPUL: I have a friend just like you. He's a good fellow. When I see you, I keep remembering him.
DRIVER: I have to pee. Where's the toilet?
UPUL: The toilet is on the other side.

The driver leaves the room. Upul takes a bottle of brandy from his bag and places it on the table. The driver enters shaking water off his wet trouser.

DRIVER: That tap is leaking. The stop valve doesn't work.

UPUL: I guess it's OK to tell you. But if my family knew I lived in such conditions they would insist on taking me home. That's a fact. But I like a free and independent life. So, for a short time I will live like this.

Upul hands the driver a glass full of brandy. He takes it, lowering his head in a humble gesture, sits down in the chair and drinks it in one gulp. Upul raises his glass and takes a sip.

DRIVER: Sir, gentlemen like you ...

UPUL: Don't call me sir. Let's drink. Have some more.

DRIVER: (*A trifle shamefacedly pours brandy into a glass.*) It seemed as if it was going to rain this afternoon but it's not likely to rain now.

UPUL: I wish it would rain continuously, non-stop for seven days.

DRIVER: Oh no. The drains will all overflow and flood the streets.

UPUL: Then everyday won't be the same. There'll be a difference. Why what's the problem?

DRIVER: Nothing.

He lowers his head smiles and once more empties his glass. Upul sips his drink.

UPUL: If the sun that rises every day does not rise on one day wouldn't that be good?

DRIVER: That would be great!

UPUL: (*pushing the bottle towards the driver*) Have some more.

Upul goes to the window.

How long is it since you've been at this house?

DRIVER: My education stopped half way. I was very keen at the time to study computers. There was no way I could afford to do it. So, then I learned to drive a car.

UPUL: Do you go about in the car alone with the lady?

DRIVER: Yes, Madam mostly travels around with me.

UPUL: Does she like music?

DRIVER: The TV and radio are on constantly in the house. Do you know to work with computers, sir?

UPUL: Yes, we do everything with them. I'll bring my computer here some time or I'll take you to my office one day. You have no problem coming there have you? Is there a special day when you drive the lady shopping?

DRIVER: There's no special day. Madam goes shopping whenever she feels like it.

UPUL: What are her favorite shops where she goes most often?

DRIVER: There are two places in Bambalapitiya and Kollupitiya. She never fails to go to those two.

Upul pours more brandy into his glass.

Tell your lady that I said she was beautiful.

The driver stares wide eyed at Upul. Upul smiles, sips his brandy and picks up his guitar.

UPUL: Tell your lady I said so.

(*Upul sings strumming his guitar.*)

Show me the way to find you
I have no one
Each night without you
is a torment.
All I do is wait
for the sun to rise again.
Where will I meet you?
on the pavement, in a bus or the train
at Majestic City or on Galle Road?
Where will I meet you?
Show me the way to find you
I have no one.

DRIVER: That's a great song. There's another song just like that one—Who is it by? Who sings it? I can't remember now. That is a great song.

UPUL: We'll sing that one too. Try to remember it.

Ravi enters carrying a parcel of food.

This is my friend Ravi. He's at the University.

The driver looks down and smiles. Ravi takes no notice.

Will you have some more brandy?

DRIVER: Oh no. That's enough.

Upul empties his glass in one gulp.

UPUL: Let's step outside.

DRIVER: If I study computers it won't be too difficult to get a good job, don't you think?

Upul puts his arm around the driver and leads him outside. Ravi stares at the two departing figures, sits at the table opens his packet of food and begins to eat. Upul returns.

RAVI: Who was that man?

UPUL: Why?

RAVI: I'd like to know
UPUL: Why?

Upul pours some brandy into his glass.

RAVI: I think the time has come to end my dealings with you.
UPUL: I on my part have no such thoughts.
RAVI: I now know the kind of a man you are.
UPUL: I, on the other hand, do not still know myself.
RAVI: You always turn the conversation to your advantage.
UPUL: Where did you have lunch today? At the University canteen?

Ravi says nothing and continues to eat. Upul takes his glass of brandy and walks to the window.

UPUL: When one eats every day from a fast food joint one longs for a home cooked meal. After a time home cooked food must taste like food from a fast food joint. That's perhaps why my father drinks till he's drunk and then goes to sleep without eating.

Silence.

UPUL: Have I told you about my father? Do you know about my two unmarried sisters? Do you know how we move from pillar to post unable to pay the rent? All you know about me is that I try to make love to the girls here. If I stop to think about my life the night will not be long enough to weep.

Upul empties his glass of brandy in one gulp and moves to the table.

Do you know how many jobs I've done just these past two months? For two weeks last month I sold cellular phones. The day the government ministers came to town they closed all the roads. There were no buses, so I had to stay in the room remember? That day I had to pay in the money on two phones I had sold. When I went the next day to pay it the owner said I had broken my trust. He said he thought I had taken the money and given him the slip. When I tried to explain what had happened he said that "fellows like me can't be trusted."

Ravi has finished his meal takes his food parcel and leaves the room. Upul pours more brandy into his glass takes a letter out of his purse and reads. Ravi returns, drinks some water from the bottle, takes a book and lies down on his bed.

UPUL: Mother has sent another letter today addressed to our former room. She says something she's never said before. That if I have a girl friend or if I'm thinking about one I should tell them. She says, "Son don't trouble your head about the problems at home." She writes like this because of a deep sadness and also a little prick of anger.

Silence.

UPUL: Do you think that you can have a better life than your parents have had? I for one doubt my mother ever lived. I think all they did was to bring us up. All I want is to do something to earn some money so that I can let my mother and family savor life even for one day. I don't want anything more.
RAVI: I don't believe that having money alone makes life …
UPUL: Don't talk rubbish.
RAVI: I'm telling you what I think.
UPUL: Think anything you like but don't talk nonsense.
RAVI: I said what I thought,
UPUL: Someday you will understand the truth about what you think of as living.
RAVI: Why? Do you think I don't live? Upul do you hear me? You say I …
UPUL: Not you, I.

There is a knock on the door.

UPUL: Our friend must have come.
RAVI: Who?
UPUL: The man who was just here.
RAVI: Who was he?
UPUL: The driver in the house upstairs.
RAVI: So, what about him?
UPUL: He's come again.
RAVI: Why?
UPUL: Ask him when he comes in.
RAVI: Don't bring that guy in here.
UPUL: Why?
RAVI: If you want to talk to him go outside and talk.
UPUL: Why? What's your reason?
RAVI: How did you get to know the man?
UPUL: I smiled at him when I went out in the morning. When I returned in the evening I talked to him.
RAVI: What did you tell him?
UPUL: I told him that we were the gentlemen who had recently rented this room.
RAVI: What else?
UPUL: I gave the man a pack of cigarettes too.
RAVI: What more?

There is a knock at the door.

UPUL: Don't worry I won't bring him into the room.

Upul leaves the room. Ravi watches him go and moves to the window. Upul returns and walks up and down agitated.

RAVI: What does the man say?
UPUL: That we must pay the next month's rent tomorrow.
RAVI: What has he to do with it?
UPUL: If not he who else?
RAVI: Who came?
UPUL: The landlord.

Silence.

UPUL: Do you have any money?
RAVI: I'm leaving tomorrow.

A knock at the door.

RAVI: Did you promise to pay him tomorrow?
UPUL: I said nothing.
RAVI: Then?
UPUL: He talked. I listened.
RAVI: Then why is he knocking again?
UPUL: He may have changed his mind and decided to ask for the money next month instead of tomorrow.
RAVI: Go find out.
UPUL: I went once. Now it's your turn.
RAVI: I'm leaving tomorrow.

The knocking continues.

UPUL: Let's just be quiet as if we are fast asleep.

Upul lies down on his bed.

RAVI: He is not going to believe that you fell asleep so fast. He may think that something has happened to us and may try to jump in through the window.
UPUL: Let him come.
RAVI: Then what?
UPUL: Let's just be quiet.

More knocking at the door. Ravi is ill at ease.

RAVI: Upul this won't work.
UPUL: That's why I said

RAVI: What?
UPUL: That you should go talk to him.
RAVI: I told you once before, tomorrow I'm …

Upul starts up from his bed.

UPUL: Yes go. Go early morning so I never set eyes on you again.

Upul leaves the room. Ravi sits at the table and stares at it. Upul returns very upset. He pours a glass of brandy, fills it to the top and gulps it all down.

I'm coming with you tomorrow.

RAVI: Did he say we must leave if we don't pay him tomorrow? What did he say?
UPUL: That they were going to beat us up and we should be careful.
RAVI: Why beat us? What have we done? Tell the man that we have already paid for 28 more days in this month.
UPUL: What?
RAVI: Look at this. The two of us have paid this guy two thousand rupees a month just for the room and that without meals.
UPUL: It wasn't the landlord.
RAVI: Who then?
UPUL: The driver from the house upstairs.
RAVI: So, what is he going to beat us up for?
UPUL: They said that if we caused trouble, they were going to inform the police that we were terrorists and put us in jail.
RAVI: He's probably trying to frighten us with this talk and get a packet of cigarettes off you every day.

Upul takes a pack of cigarettes out of his pocket and throws it at Ravi.

Is he demanding a bottle of arrack?

Silence.

UPUL: Let's leave right now.

Upul begins to stuff clothes into his bag.

RAVI: Where are you going?
UPUL: Somewhere, anywhere.
RAVI: If the police catch us and ask where we are going at this time of night I may never get back my identity card, once they take it.
UPUL: What if the police come here tonight?
RAVI: Why would they come here?
UPUL: They had said they were going to send the police tonight.

RAVI: Who? Why?

Upul goes to Ravi.

UPUL: Please tell me quickly what I should do? I'm totally innocent man, save me.
RAVI: What did you do?
UPUL: I did nothing.

Upul grabs his bag. Clutches it and sits on the bed looking down.

RAVI: You can't have done nothing. You have done some …
UPUL: I didn't do anything.
RAVI: Don't lie to me.
UPUL: No, it's true.
RAVI: What was it?
UPUL: I didn't do anything.
RAVI: Then what the hell is this about?

Silence.

UPUL: I asked him
RAVI: Who is him?
UPUL: The fellow who was here just now,
RAVI: So, what of him?
UPUL: The man upstairs had seen him come in here this evening.
RAVI: So what?
UPUL: The letter I had given him to give to the woman …
RAVI: What woman?
UPUL: The one who was upstairs, last evening.
RAVI: What …?
UPUL: Why, damn you, the one who was there yesterday.
RAVI: Was it that young girl?
UPUL: Who?

Silence.

RAVI: What I am saying is …
UPUL: That she is not yet married?
RAVI: Not that …
UPUL: Then what?
RAVI: He has no right to threaten you.
UPUL: Do you know who he is?
RAVI: Whoever he may be, I say he has no right to threaten you.
UPUL: Will he kill me?

RAV': Why would he kill you? Did you threaten violence against him? I'm asking you?

UPUL: Even if I wanted to do something can he kill me for that?

RAVI: The answer to your question is, if you argue on the concept of your rights the case is against you.

UPUL: Are you saying that if I fall in love with a woman who legally belongs to you, that you can kill me for it?

Silence.

If something were to happen to me my folks at home won't even have a chance of getting some form of compensation.

What will the women whom I said I loved think when they hear of this.

Perhaps the only one who will miss me is the woman who sells roasted gram by the beach.

Why don't you advise me? Say something. Tell me not to be upset or afraid, whatever happens—to take what comes, just swallow my dhal[4] and try to digest it. Alternatively tell me that we should beat them up.

Silence.

UPUL: Aren't you afraid? Are you leaving early tomorrow morning? Whatever one tries to do one always ends up getting beaten. That's all that happens. You are not a friend. You are a bastard. You might have told me …

Yes, let everyone just sit around and wait while we get crushed. Why can't you go to them and beg forgiveness on my behalf? Do at least that. Is there anything a friend cannot do for a friend?

RAVI: That is why it is said that there should be limits to lechery.

UPUL: Didn't you feel desire for her when you saw her?

RAVI: Those who act on every impulse are not men.

UPUL: Will they kill me like some animal? Before that happens tell me what to do. What should I do? In the past you advised me to marry the woman I loved most and to try to live happily and contentedly afterwards. Why don't you say even that? But you never asked the question why you failed to follow that advice yourself.

Upul puts the bottle of brandy to his mouth and takes several gulps. He is now partially drunk.

UPUL: If you can go find a marriage registrar who works at night bring him here. Tonight, I will get married. Then tomorrow morning for breakfast we will go to the Kandalama hotel.[5] In the afternoon we will go to some beach for a swim. However, we must get back before nightfall or I won't be able to find the bus halt to get off at this place. What do you say to that? Are you thinking, "Is this the kind of creep I have been living with?" Are you disgusted at the thought that a human being can become so debauched?

Upul suddenly falls on his bed. Ravi looks at Upul for some time then walks to the window. A moment passes. Upul suddenly lets out a groan and starts up.

UPUL: What was that noise? What was that sound?

RAVI: Can't you fall asleep?

UPUL: Where did you go? Where did you secretly try to go? I'm asking you. After having lived together the two of us, the moment I was in trouble you tried to run away didn't you? Why don't you say something?

Silence.

Shall I go find the landlord and tell him everything? But I don't know if he is a friend of that man upstairs.

Upul falls down again on his bed. Ravi lies down on his. The lights in the room change. The landlord, the man upstairs and the driver enter. The man from upstairs sees the bottle of brandy on the table and forces it down the driver's throat. The driver coughs and chokes. Upul sits up in bed and stares at them. The landlord comes up to Upul.

LANDLORD: We are very respectable people. Our neighbors are also respectable people. If I knew you were this type of person, I would not have rented the room to you.

UPUL: Please forgive me. I did not think it was serious.

LANDLORD: What?

UPUL: It had become a kind of habit with me.

LANDLORD: To do this kind of thing?

UPUL: I did not think too much about it.

LANDLORD: What does your father do for a living?

Silence.

Is there such a person?

The man from upstairs comes up to Upul:

Why do you seem amazed? You don't know anything do you?

LANDLORD: You may have a fine body but do you know that when it is broken it hurts?

The man from upstairs goes to the window.

What do you think about having a window here?

UPUL: Please don't kill me. I have not even begun to live.

MAN FROM UPSTAIRS: Has your mother not taught you not to throw stones at a honey comb but to use a better technique to extract the honey?

Silence.

Come and sit here

Upul sits in the chair.

Do you wish to make a confession?

UPUL: Each time my father spoke kindly to my mother I wept in my sleep. Why couldn't the two of them live harmoniously like that every day I asked and understood the reason long before I first kissed a woman.

There is a sound of a gunshot. Ravi struggles on his bed. The man from upstairs puts the pistol in his pocket.

UPUL: Why did you do that?

MAN FROM UPSTAIRES: Though he seemed asleep he was awake. There was the chance that he could have jumped through the window. Can you suggest a better means of precaution?

Silence.

UPUL: Aren't you going to shoot me?

MAN FROM UPSTAIRS: You should get married.

Upul sits astounded. The landlord, the man from upstairs and the driver carry Ravi out. A young woman Indira comes in. She arranges the things on the table. Upul stares at her.

INDIRA: When are we going to the dentist to get my tooth fixed? I have to buy a dress for our daughter too. My sister's wedding is next month. Did you hear me?

Indira arranges the clothes scattered on the bed and puts them away in an orderly fashion.

Today there is neither fish nor meat in the house. I wrote a list of items the day before yesterday. Remember to bring them at least today. The child's vitamins are also over.

Indira goes to the other bed.

Don't we have to pay the next year's advance rent to the landlord tomorrow? What do you think? Is there anyone you know left whom you could ask for a loan?

Indira goes up to Upul.

Upul you must think at least of the child and try to find some other means of earning a living.

Upul picks up a shirt from off the chair and wears it.

INDIRA: Don't stop to have a drink with this one and that one but come home early today before the child goes to sleep.

Indira leaves. Another young woman Dhammi enters. Upul and Dhammi sit on two chairs at the table. The driver appears as a waiter at a restaurant and places two bottles of fizzy drinks on the table. Dhammi looks on with a smile on her face.

UPUL: One day I told my wife about you. Do you know what she said? I saw her face darken, her ears redden and her eyes glower.

DHAMMI: You're a funny person.

UPUL: Why do you say that?

DHAMMI: Our Ravi is not like that.

UPUL: What do you mean by that?

DHAMMI: If that happened to me I would divorce him.

UPUL: Dhammi you mustn't get so angry. If you get so angry …

DHAMMI: What will happen?

UPUL: Men are like that.

DHAMMI: I know I'm not talking to a decent man. Now are you angry?

The two of them stare into each other's eyes.

This is not the kind of place I like. I would so love to find a nice quiet place to be able to live totally free.

UPUL: When the two of us alone, sit close, without anyone else around, looking at each other without saying a word, a river flows beside us. The fragrance of flowers gets intensified by the cold. There is a shower of rain coming towards us but we two don't move. If I find a place like that where the two of us can stay motionless I will call you.

DHAMMI: Yes please, do remember to tell me. Our Ravi will like that too.

UPUL: I'm going to the toilet. I'll be back.

Upul leaves. Ravi enters accompanied by the man from upstairs and the driver. Dhammi looks amazed. Upul enters.

UPUL: Hello Ravi. I happened to run in to Dhammi by chance. You seem to have put on some weight of late. The two of us were catching up on news.

RAVI: Aren't you still at the same place?

UPUL: Yes man! The landlord keeps telling me to find another place. But it's …

RAVI: (*to Dhammi*) Let's go.

Ravi and Dhammi prepare to leave.

UPUL: Hey Man, do you know these guys?

RAVI: No, I don't know them. Are they your friends?

UPUL: No.

RAVI: Then you should get to know them.

Ravi leaves with Dhammi. Upul also starts to leave.

THE MAN FROM UPSTAIRS: Come and sit down here.

Upul sits on a chair. The driver jumps on the table and stands there. Upul stares at him. Suddenly, the driver jumps down and gives Upul a blow. Upul falls. The man from upstairs picks him up on his back and puts him down on the bed. The landlord brings Ravi on his back and puts him down on his bed. The landlord, the gentleman upstairs and the driver leave. The stage lights that had changed now return to what they were in the beginning. Upul and Ravi are asleep. A knock at the door. Ravi wakes.

RAVI: Hey Upul! Upul!

Upul wakes with a start, opens his eyes and looks around.

RAVI: Did you hear that?

A knock at the door

UPUL: Who do you think it is? Do you think …
RAVI: Don't make a sound.

Silence.

UPUL: How much longer before it is light?

Ravi stares at the door. Upul also stares at the door. The knocking continues. Lights go out and the stage is in darkness.

The end

****

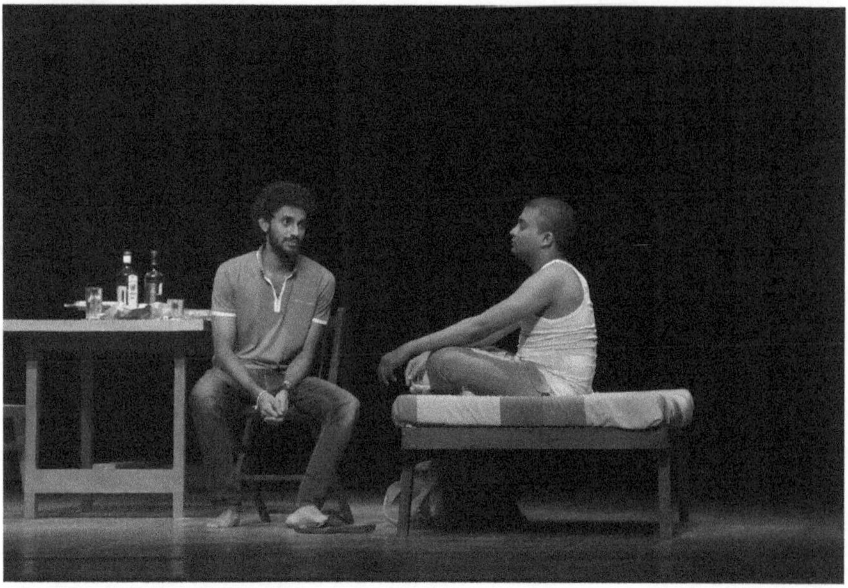

PHOTOGRAPH 5.1 Upul and Ravi in *Aren't You Going to Shoot Me?* Photograph by Hemantha Arunasiri

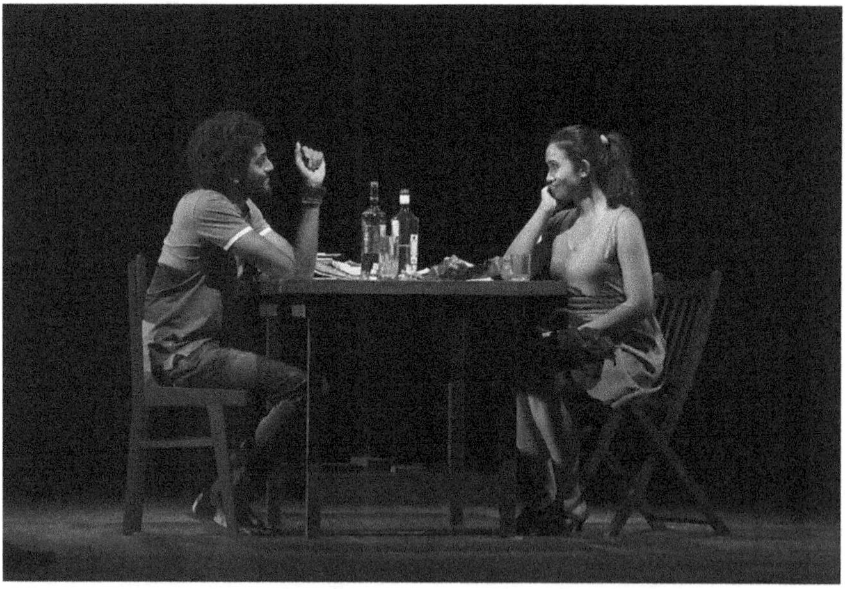

PHOTOGRAPH 5.2 Upul and Dhammi in *Aren't You Going to Shoot Me?* Photograph by Hemantha Arunasiri

Notes

1 Considered to be one of the oldest works of classical Sinhala poetry, belonging to the late twelfth century. Author unknown.
2 Chickpeas.
3 University students generally had a certain status and respect in the society. That perception has changed over the years. In the late 1980s, they were seen by certain segments in society as unemployable and were seen in a rather negative light with their constant strikes, protests and internal violence within the campuses.
4 Dhal is the poor man's food, the cheapest and most basic curry served with rice.
5 A five-star hotel where rich newly weds go for their honeymoons.

***

Rajitha Dissanayake started his career as a playwright while he was studying at the University of Colombo in the early 1990s. Even as a high school student, he was writing plays in the late 1980s. Rajitha obtained a Master of Fine Arts from the University of Sri Jayawardenapura, Sri Lanka. Rajitha's plays explore in aesthetic and human terms socio-political realities of the day. Not only is he a prolific and focused playwright and director, he has also been able to prove that one can straddle both box office success and national awards, impressing audiences, critics and panels of judges equally. Rajitha has staged his plays in India, Egypt and Europe. In 2006, he was a visiting scholar at Ball State University in Indiana, USA. He is also a visiting lecturer at several Sri Lankan Universities and is a producer of radio programs. Some of Rajitha Dissanayake's plays include *Hithala Gaththu Theeranayak/A Decision Taken with Much Thought* (2018), *Nathuwa Bari Minihek/An Indisposable Man* (2016), *Apasu Herenne Be/No Return* (2008) and *Veeraya Merila/The Hero is Dead* (2002).